# MATERNITY POLICIES AND WORKING WOMEN

# MATERNITY POLICIES AND WORKING WOMEN

Sheila B. Kamerman,
Alfred J. Kahn, and
Paul Kingston

Columbia University Press
New York   1983

Library of Congress Cataloging in Publication Data

Kamerman, Sheila B.
  Maternity policies and working women.

  Includes bibliographical references and index.
  1. Maternity leave—United States.  2. Insurance,
Maternity—United States.  I. Kahn, Alfred J.,
1919–    .  II. Kingston, Paul W.  III. Title.
HD6065.5.U6K35  1983    331.4'25763    83-7624
ISBN 0-231-05750-4

Columbia University Press
New York   Guildford, Surrey

Clothbound editions of Columbia University Press books are Smyth-
sewn and printed on permanent and durable acid-free paper.

*For all our children, who are of varied ages, but who depend upon a society which takes parenting seriously.*

# CONTENTS

Acknowledgments                                                    ix

1. Maternity and the Working Woman                                  1

2. Historical Notes on Maternity Policies in the United
   States                                                          29

3. The Benefit Picture: Employee and Employer Perspectives                                                       47

4. The Benefit Picture: State and Federal Provisions               77

5. Maternity Policies in Private Industry: The Operating
   Picture                                                         99

6. Maternity Policies: Trends and Issues                          133

   Appendix. Maternity Benefits in the Private Sector:
   Study Design and Methodology                                   161

   Notes                                                          175

   Index                                                          181

# ACKNOWLEDGMENTS

With gratitude to the W. T. Grant Foundation, which understood the connection between maternity policy and child development.

Our special thanks and appreciation go to the many companies that cooperated with us in helping to develop this first national picture of maternity policies in the U.S., and to the hundreds of individuals who responded to our questionnaire and to our telephone interviews. Most of all we want to thank those working women we interviewed who talked freely and feelingly of their own experiences, sharing with us and with you their personal and work lives and their insights. We hope that in some small way, what we have written may make a difference.

Sheila B. Kamerman
Alfred J. Kahn
Paul W. Kingston

# MATERNITY POLICIES AND WORKING WOMEN

# 1. MATERNITY AND THE WORKING WOMAN

"These girls have it easy today, and they don't even know it. Six weeks paid leave and another three months unpaid if they want it with their jobs saved for them."

She spoke brusquely and she seemed angry and resentful. Assistant director of her department, with the company for ten years, she had been urged by her boss to talk to us as a woman and as a manager about the company's maternity policies. And so she did: she described the benefits, what the experience of the firm was in providing them, and what some of the problems were. But more revealingly, at some point as she talked, she began to reminisce.

Eleanor Jamison had worked all of her adult life and she was now close to retirement. She had been married and had brought up three children at a time when most women, and certainly most mothers, were at home and not at work. She talked about what it was like to be a woman and a wife at the workplace thirty years ago, what it was like to become pregnant and be working at the same time, what it was like to be a mother and to continue working. Finally, she discussed what it was like now to be a manager with women working under her with a very different view of what the work world was like and what they expected of it.

"Why, when I got married in 1940," she recalled, "I needed permission from my boss to remain on the job. Not only were there no benefits provided, nor any kind of medical or sickness insurance, but there was even some question as to whether a married woman should be allowed to work! Then World War

II came along, and the bosses were glad to have women like me. After the war it was different. They only let me stay because I had been there a long time."

"But when I got pregnant in 1947," she continued, "I didn't even bother to tell the boss I was pregnant. I knew he would never let me stay. I just announced I was leaving."

She stayed home with her baby for two years and then, because her husband was going into a new business, they decided she should go back to work in order to have a steady source of income while her husband got established. Her second child was born in 1952.

"I had a better job then, and a better boss. I told him when I got pregnant, and he let me work until my sixth month and then said I had to leave. That wasn't too bad because a lot of women I knew were made to leave as soon as they showed, often in their third month. It was very tough for a woman with a family to support in those days. I asked my employer for a leave, but he refused. He said I just had to take my chances. There was nothing else I could do. But as soon as I was ready to come back, one month after the baby was born, he let me."

"When I got pregnant with my third child in 1957, I was still working for the same people. This time, they let me work until six weeks before the baby was due and then told me I had to leave, but they still wouldn't give me a maternity leave even though I asked for it. I had been working for them for over eight years, and they knew I would come back. I was so angry that I stayed out for six months that time, even though I knew they needed me and they wanted me back. But I got back at them before I came back." She reported with some pride, "I made them give me a good raise."

"I've managed all right. It was hard, and there was no insurance. It is very different today for the girls who get pregnant. They have health insurance and disability benefits and job-protected child care leaves. And it is not easy for an employer to manage if an employee is out for a few months, yet some of these girls still complain."

Not all young women have the current protection Eleanor Jamison described.

"Nobody cared, and nobody noticed," one young woman told us. "I worked right up to the last day. I called in sick when my pains began. Then I went to the hospital and had my baby. I was home in four days, and one week later I was back on the job. I needed the money. That was two days more sick leave than I had. They told me that they would advance me the other two days, but I had better not get sick again—at least not for a while. My ma is taking care of the baby for me now." This was the matter-of-fact statement of a young single mother, three months after her baby was born.

This book is about maternity policies in the United States today, about the rights some working women have and the benefits they receive from their employers when they are pregnant and when they give birth:

— the health and medical insurance that covers hospital and physicians costs;
— the job-related leave, with seniority and pension rights protected;
— the wage replacement when they are out on leave;
— the other provisions that make maternity manageable for women who work.

Certainly the picture is very different from what it was forty or thirty or even ten years ago. But is it really as rosy as Eleanor Jamison seemed to think? Or as dreadful as the other young woman suggested?

Are working women, their families, and their babies protected at the time of childbirth? What kind of protection exists, for whom, and how good is it? Are maternity benefits very costly? Do maternity leaves create problems for employers at the workplace? And if so, how do they manage? How important are maternity benefits anyway—for women, for children, for families, and for the rest of us?

The purpose of this book is to explore what maternity policies for working women exist in this country. (For the moment, we do not attend to the needs of women who do not work outside the home.) Many people seem to assume that almost all working women today are protected at the time of childbirth: that their medical costs are covered, that they are entitled to a job-protected leave for a reasonable period of time, and that their income is assured, too, through some kind of insurance benefit or salary continuation plan. Sadly, that view is wrong.

Unlike seventy-five other countries, including all other advanced industrialized societies and many among the less developed countries, the United States has no statutory provision that guarantees a woman the right to a leave from employment for a specified period, protects her job while she is on leave, and provides a cash benefit equal to all or a significant portion of her wage while she is not working because of pregnancy and childbirth. Nor does the United States guarantee a working mother the right to health insurance to cover her own medical expenses at the time of pregnancy and childbirth as well as those of her child. Benefits such as these cover most employed women in other countries and play an essential role in maternal and child health care, as well as in protecting family income at a critical time in the family life cycle.

It is not that the United States has no national maternity policy at all. Since October 1978, such a policy (or at least one part of a policy) has been in place. That policy is to require that employers treat pregnancy and maternity the same as any other illness or disability, and that employers treat their women employees who become pregnant or give birth to a child just as they would treat a man who is temporarily disabled or ill. Thus, if an employer provides paid sick leave or disability leave for male employees, the employer must make the same benefits available to female workers before or after childbirth. Federal law does not, however, require that employers provide special benefits covering illness or disability; the only requirement is that for those employers who do so, the same protection must be available with regard to maternity and pregnancy.

Other private and public provisions, inconsistently available, must also be counted as part of our policy. Federal employees are entitled to certain benefits at the time of maternity, as are most state employees. Five states (California, Hawaii, New Jersey, New York, Rhode Island) and Puerto Rico provide statutory benefits for working women at childbirth. Moreover, a large number of private employers offer some benefits, usually basic hospitalization insurance. Some employers permit employees to take an unpaid leave and hold their jobs for them. Far fewer provide some kind of cash benefit or wage replacement.

The finding of this book is that protection—from either public or private sources—is not nearly as extensive as most people think. Many women have few if any benefits. For most, the benefits that are available are much less generous than is commonly thought. There is a substantial range in what employers provide and, therefore, in what working women are entitled to. Moreover, the fact that a very small group of states ensures maternity benefits for almost all their working women creates further inequities based on where a woman works. Finally, serious unresolved problems exist because of the specific policy instrument used in this country and the definition of pregnancy and maternity carried with it. This device, the use of disability or sickness benefits, carries a connotation that has been permitted to distort the meaning of maternity. The larger meaning of maternity as motherhood has been ignored in this country, and the serious limitations of U.S. maternity policy are not yet widely understood.

We begin by discussing why maternity benefits are important. Our theme here is that given the growing numbers of working women—working wives and working mothers—the likelihood of an employed woman becoming pregnant is very high. Indeed, 85 percent of working women are likely to become pregnant during their working lives. Many of these women will remain at work after they give birth, and the percentage doing so is growing steadily. Over half of those who work while pregnant are back at work within less than a year after childbirth. Clearly, there are implications in this for maternal and child health, for mother-child relationships, for family economic security, and for job and career development. Although maternity benefits may not generally be an important component of employee benefit packages for pregnant woman workers, for their children and for their families, they are or can be an enormously critical benefit.

In chapter 2 we present a picture of what our current national policy is, and how and why the federal legislation evolved. Our country's maternity policy stems neither from a firm base in health policy nor from protective legislation or child welfare provision. Rather, it is related historically to civil rights legislation, the women's movement, and the growth of American social policy generally. More specifically, it emerged as an issue in sex discrimination and then as a response to it. Federal pregnancy and maternity policy clearly accomplished some immediate and important protection for women, but it left some larger issues completely outside the debate. That sex discrimination is an important aspect of the maternity policy debate is accurate. That it is not the whole issue and that it should not define the boundaries of the maternity discussion is part of our ultimate thesis.

In chapter 3 we review the situation today for women workers. What maternity protection is provided, by what kind of employers, for what kind of employees? Our major focus is on the policies of private employers. We supplement our own survey with data from other studies. In chapter 4 we continue with discussion of what is available at the state level in the five states that mandate benefits. Our goal is to provide the most up-to-date picture of maternity benefits available, the women who are entitled to them, and those who are not.

Chapter 5 presents our analysis of the current situation, enriched by in-depth pictures of specific companies and the benefits they provide, as well as of particular women workers and their personal experiences. We explore the problems that exist and the issues involved in responding to unmet needs. We then raise questions for policy in both the public and private sectors.

Finally, in chapter 6, we explore alternative approaches to the maternity policy issue in the United States and some possible solutions to the problems that have emerged.

## ARE MATERNITY POLICIES IMPORTANT?

In our society the pairing of maternity and policy has a strange, perhaps disquieting, ring. By contrast, retirement policies are recognized as critical to any discussion of how to protect people in their old age, provide opportunities for young workers, and assure those who have worked all their lives the reward of some period of supported leisure. Similarly, apprenticeship and training policies are widely recognized as necessary to facilitate the entry of young workers into the labor force. Others insist on the importance of policies that assure individuals equality of opportunity in the job market and the career ladder. All of these, in short, are policy fields that significant numbers of people consider both distinguishable and important. Yet there are many who question whether there is any reason to have a policy or policies on working women at the time of their pregnancy and maternity, except perhaps to provide them with health and medical insurance coverage. "Besides," such doubters protest, "most women stop work when they get pregnant and don't go back until their children are in school." That view ignores the reality of the contemporary American work force and the strains involved in meshing work and family lives.

## Working Wives and Mothers

One of the most dramatic changes in the last two decades has been the growth in labor force participation rates of women, especially married women with children.[1] In 1960, approximately 27 percent of all wives were employed or seeking employment outside the home. By 1970, this figure was almost 40 percent and by 1980, 54 percent (and 56 percent in 1982), more than doubling in a little over two decades. Indeed, the rate of increase during the 1970s (36 percent) reflected an even sharper rise than during the 1960s and has signaled something like a real revolution in family life styles, in child rearing, and in the patterns of daily life generally.

Single mothers, especially divorced and separated women, have always had a high labor force participation rate. Their employment rates have risen only slightly, from 59 percent in 1970 to 66 percent in 1980 (and 67.7 percent in 1982). However, the absolute numbers of female-headed families with children have increased substantially over the decade, from about 10 percent of all families with children in 1970 to over 18 percent in 1981. This represents a rise of 93 percent in the absolute number of female-headed households in just eleven years. In conjunction with greater labor force participation rates of women, that increase affects the living experience of even larger numbers of mothers and children.

The increase in labor force participation has been even more dramatic among mothers with very young children. Half the mothers of preschool-aged children, including 57 percent of the mothers of children aged 3 to 5, and 46 percent of the mothers of children under 3 were working in 1982. The comparable figure for mothers of preschool-aged children in 1970 was 32 percent. In 1975, the earliest year in which data for labor force participation rates of mothers of very young children (under age 3) were published, the rate was 34 percent. (See table 1.1 and 1.2.) The most astonishing development in the course of the decade has been the entry into the labor force of young, married women, under age 35, with children under age 3. Forty-four percent of these women worked in 1981, as compared with 26 percent in 1970. Two-thirds of these women worked full time; one-quarter worked full time all year round.

Viewing these developments from the perspective of the children, by 1979 more than half of all children in the United States had working mothers. By 1980 that was true even for most children living in two-parent families (53 percent in 1981). Moreover, this kind of family pattern is becoming increasingly typical for very young children. Forty-six percent of the children under age 6 had working mothers in 1981, contrasted with 29 percent a decade ago. Even more dramatic has been the increase in the proportion of children under age 3 who have working mothers, from 32 percent in 1976 to 42 percent in 1981, only five years later.

## Other Developments

Four other trends point to the importance of maternity policies for working women and are critical to recognize in evaluating present policies.

*Fewer Children*[2]. First is the fact that the fertility rate for women has declined significantly. Births to date for wives aged 18 to 34 declined from 2.1 in 1967 and 1.7 in 1973 to 1.5 in

**Table 1.1.** Labor Force Status of Women with Children Under Age 3

| With Children | 1975 | | | 1979 | | | 1981 | | |
|---|---|---|---|---|---|---|---|---|---|
| | All Women | Married | Single | All Women | Married | Single | All Women | Married | Single |
| Under age 3 | 34.3 | 32.5 | 43.4 | 42.8 | 38.9 | 49.0 | 44.3 | 43.7 | 47.7 |
| Under age 2 | 31.2 | 30.4 | 38.5 | 41.0 | 37.0 | 45.4 | 42.2 | 41.8 | 42.9 |
| Under age 1* | 31.7 | 27.2 | 40.3 | 35.8 | 33.4 | 41.2 | — | — | — |
| 6-11 months* | 30.4 | 29.3 | 43.3 | 38.5 | 37.1 | 45.5 | — | — | — |
| 0-5 months* | 26.8 | 24.9 | 37.7 | 31.0 | 29.5 | 37.2 | — | — | — |

SOURCE: Unpublished data provided by Dr. Martin O'Connell, Fertility Division, Bureau of the Census.
*Women aged 18 to 34.

**Table 1.2.** Children Under Age 2 with Working
Mothers

| 1975 | | 1981 | |
|---|---|---|---|
| Hus/Wife | Female Head | Hus/Wife | Female Head |
| 30.7 | 38.4 | 41.2 | 41.5 |

SOURCE: Unpublished data, Bureau of Labor Statistics.

1979. For this same age group, lifetime expected births dropped from 3 to 2.2 over these same years. The fertility rate for *working* wives is still lower (40.9 per 1,000 in 1980 compared with 130.1 per 1,000 for women not in the paid labor force). Thus, although the two-child family remains typical for the society at large, some employed women will have only one child. This is especially true for the growing numbers of women who are deferring marriage and childbirth until becoming established in their careers. A decline and relative stability in the numbers of children that women are bearing make the costs of providing maternity benefits both more predictable and less costly.*

*Women Contribute to Family Income.* Clearly, for women who head their own families, earned income is essential. The contribution made by working wives in two-parent families to family income, although not of the same weight as that made by husbands, also is of growing importance. Overall, working wives now contribute about 26 percent of family income (compared with 20 percent in 1970). However, more than half the wives aged 25 to 34, the peak childbearing years, now work full time, all year. Women who work full time all year round contribute 39 percent of the family income, and the proportion of women following this pattern is increasing.

Furthermore, of particular importance to our discussion, not only are more women working today, but they are continuing to work despite pregnancy, maternity, and the demands of child

*The higher fertility rate for women not in the labor force reflects in part the recent childbearing of women who have temporarily dropped out of the labor force to have a child.

care and child rearing. More and more women are planning to begin work or return to work shortly after the birth of a child. Indeed, many young women never really leave the labor force today, or leave it only briefly at the time of childbirth.

*Patterns of Employment During Pregnancy.* No longer do women feel they have to make a choice between staying at work and becoming pregnant. Among women who gave birth between 1970 and 1973, 42 percent worked for some portion of their pregnancy and half of these women worked during the last trimester. This proportion varied widely, depending on the order of birth and other factors.

For women giving birth to a first child, 61 percent worked; for women giving birth to a second child, 36 percent, and for third and subsequent births, 28 percent. Regardless of birth order, the older the woman was at the time of childbirth, the more likely she was to work during her pregnancy. Similarly, women with higher levels of education were also more likely to work while pregnant. Over the decade, fewer women are having more than two children; the educational level for women has risen, and the median age for childbearing has increased. The likely trend, therefore, even apart from the significant increase in the proportion of women of this age working, is for a much larger group to be working while pregnant, including working during the last trimester.

*Patterns of Employment After Childbirth.* Childbirth no longer means a lengthy absence or even complete disengagement from the labor force. Among those women who worked during pregnancy, between 1970 and 1973, most (62 percent) returned to work within less than two years after childbirth, according to a 1973 survey. This number, however, includes women who gave birth only a few weeks before the survey as well as those who gave birth two to three years earlier. Of the women who worked during their pregnancy, 10 percent had returned to work by the second month following childbirth, more than 25 percent by the fourth month, more than 33 percent by the sixth month, and 50 percent by the end of the first year.[3]

More recently, a June 1978 survey showed that of the 17.2

million wives 18 to 34 years old, 51 percent were employed.[4] Seventy-five percent of the 4.4 million wives who had never had a child were working; the corresponding percentage for the 12.8 million wives who had had a child, though considerably lower, was still a substantial 43 percent. Older married mothers (30 to 34) were more likely to be working than the younger mothers (18 to 24), but in large measure this probably reflected the older age of their children. With children of the same age, younger mothers are more likely to be at work outside the home than older ones. Thus, young wives (under 30) are more likely to be working when their children are under age 3 (43 percent) than older wives (37 percent). In general, the youngest wives in the group were far more likely to be in the labor force than the older wives, although they also had a much higher rate of unemployment.

Of the 2.5 million wives who were 18 to 34 years old at the time of the 1978 survey *and* had given birth to a child within one year of the survey, 34 percent were in the labor force. Among wives whose youngest child was 2 years old, 46 percent were in the labor force. In 1979 the percentage of women with a child under 1 year who were in the labor force rose to 35 percent and in 1980 to 38 percent. In 1981, of all women 18 to 44 years old who had a child in the previous twelve-month period, 42 percent were in the labor force. The trend for women with very young children to be working is especially dramatic when we look at the last five years. Labor force participation rates of mothers of children aged 3 have increased by about 10 percent (from 45 to 51 percent) between 1977 and 1982, and by a similar percentage for those a little older, but an astonishing one-third (from 32 to almost 42 percent) for mothers of children under 1 year.[5] In short, the working young mother with small children has become common.

## THE IMPORTANCE OF THE FIRST YEAR OF LIFE

Given the diversity of infants, parents, and life circumstances, no serious student of current child development research would make categorical assertions as to what is always best for children and their parents. On the other hand, few would dispute Belsky's summary of the following three themes as characterizing current knowledge: "(1) The extended dependency period of the human infant and the opportunity this offers for early learning; (2) the bidirectional nature of caregiver-infant influence; and (3) the significance of infancy for later development." [6]

The newborn is only partially formed, and much of what occurs in early months is in some sense by way of completion. The smoothness of routines and character of the environment are of major significance in regulating physiological responses. A cooperative caretaker who interacts sensitively helps with early tension management. A responsive loving adult is essential if the infant is to effectuate critical attachments. [7] What occurs during the first nine or twelve months may not determine all that occurs later, but it determines what the child brings to future life transactions and thus is enormously influential.

Clearly, there are other-than-parental caretakers. The research on parental work and child care does not suggest that mothers cannot safely be members of the labor force or plan on use of child care programs. [8] Nonetheless, what is known about early infancy (and what is uncertain) does generally suggest that both parents should not hurry the return to work after childbirth or to use external care arrangements in the early weeks. All other factors need consideration, of course, but the early weeks and months of a child's life are a critical time for familial and societal investment in the opportunity for direct care by parents. Individual preferences and circumstances will surely incline some to alternatives, and there is no suggestion that these will have any catastrophic effects. Child development, nonetheless, depends on sustained, concentrated interaction with a loving caretaker, and it is difficult to conceive of a better societal strategy than one that permits parental involvement.

In short, while the research results are not always definitive, it would appear that the ability of a parent to devote himself or herself to the child, without excessive diversion or external pressure, can have important consequences for (1) a good physical start including less mortality in the first year; (2) cognitive-perceptual and socio-emotional development; and (3) emotional bonding and attachment, with its long-range implications for personality and character.[9] When individual resources or social policy can make it possible, it is a good strategy to ensure a joint child-parent start for a period of at least three to nine months, even though parental circumstances might then require labor force participation of both parents, or a single parent, and alternative child care arrangements.[10] Three months seem like very little, given the knowledge of the phases of development in the first six or nine months—but three months is far closer to the target than two or three weeks! Most countries in the world have come much closer to this target than we have.

## WHAT OTHER COUNTRIES PROVIDE: AN OVERVIEW[11]

Three benefits are paramount in any discussion of maternity-related policies in other countries:

1. Health and medical insurance for mother and child, including coverage of hospital and physician expenses during pregnancy, at the time of childbirth, and for postnatal care.
2. The right of an employed woman to a leave from work for a specified period at the time of childbirth, with the assurance of job protection as well as protection of seniority, pension entitlements, and other fringe benefits.
3. A cash benefit paid to the woman during this leave, provided through the social insurance or social security system, or by the employer, and equal to all or a portion of the insured wage, for a similarly specified period.

The latter two benefits together, the guaranteed job-protected leave and the cash benefit to replace wages, constitute what is usually described as the *statutory maternity leave policy*. In a few countries, all or part of this benefit may be shared by fathers. When the sharing is for a small portion of an overall leave entitlement, the benefit still tends to be called a maternity leave; when fathers and mothers can share equally, that is, when either parent may be eligible, the benefit is termed parental leave or parental benefit.

Seventy-five countries, including many developing countries and every industrialized country *except* the United States, provide some variation of the statutory maternity leave or parental benefit. Sixteen countries that do not have a national health insurance or a national sickness benefit insurance nevertheless provide statutory maternity leaves.

Among the more industrialized countries, the minimum paid leave is twelve weeks. The International Labor Organization recommended this as a standard as far back as 1919 to include six weeks before and six weeks after childbirth. Increasingly, fourteen weeks (eight weeks after birth) is becoming the minimum, and the modal pattern in Europe today is about five months. The maximum is twelve months in Sweden, provided as a parental benefit available to both mothers and fathers, with a generous payment for nine months and (recently) an added token payment for three months more. (See table 1.3 for an overview of provision in selected countries.)

Most countries permit some portion of the leave to be taken before expected parturition, usually six weeks; but sometimes, as in Britain and Canada, as much as eleven weeks is permitted. Several countries mandate two to six weeks before expected birth and/or six weeks after. Where prenatal leave is mandated, extensions are provided if the birth occurs later than anticipated. Some countries provide additional leave under special circumstances: for second and subsequent children, for multiple births, or for single mothers. All countries provide leave extensions in cases of difficult pregnancies or deliveries. Regardless of what is provided, most countries leave the decision to use the benefit and how much to use to the individual woman or parent.

Most countries provide a benefit equal to 100 percent of insured wages (the maximum wage covered under social insurance) or 90 percent (that wage less social insurance contributions). In Canada and Israel the benefit is equal to only a portion of the insured wage (60 and 75 percent, respectively). In the Federal Republic of Germany the maximum grant provided by the government is equal to about 77 percent of the average female wage in 1979; in addition, employers are mandated to supplement this benefit up to the woman's full wage (if wages are

**Table 1.3.** Maternity and Parental Leaves—Basic Data, 1982

| Country | Eligibility or Qualifying Conditions | Duration of Leave | Benefit Level or Rate | Financing | Job Security | Additional Benefits |
|---------|-----|-----|-----|-----|-----|-----|
| Austria | Natural and adoptive mothers qualify with 52 wks in last 2 yrs in covered employment (20 wks for mothers under 21).<br><br>Exclusions: casual labor. | 8 wks before confinement; 8 wks after birth (12 wks in special cases) mandated. | 100% of weekly earnings, up to maximum insured wage. | Contributory: 50% from government; 25% employer; 25% employee.<br><br>Employer and employee contributions are the same: 31.5% of wages, 2.5% of salaries. | Same or comparable job guaranteed. Seniority and pension rights protected. | Supplementary unpaid leave up to 1 yr is available to all mothers after paid maternity leave. Benefit level is flat rate, higher for single mothers than for married women, provided under unemployment insurance and financed the same way. Full job protection and pension rights guaranteed but not seniority. |
| Canada | Natural mothers only. Maternity Leave: federal legislation covers 10% of labor force, provides right to leave | Leave: Federal legislation provides 17 wks; 11 wks before expected birth and 6 wks after; provincial | 60% of previous insured wages up to maximum insured wage, payable after 2 wks waiting period | Contributory: employee, 1.35%; employer, 1.4% × employee premiums. | Federal legislation guarantees job, pension, and seniority; provincial legislation varies. | If no job at end of maternity leave, have right to convert to regular unemployment insurance. |

work for women employed in covered employment for at least 1 yr. Most employed women are under jurisdiction of provincial codes instead. Maternity Cash Benefit: Provided under federal unemployment insurance program (covers 91% of labor force) to all women who (1) worked at least 20 wks in covered employment in last year or since commencing use of unemployment insurance and (2) worked at least 10 wks in covered employment between thirtieth and fiftieth wks before expected childbirth.

legislation varies. Cash benefit: 15 wks.

from any time between 8 wks before expected birth to 17 wks after birth.

**Table 1.3.** Maternity and Parental Leaves—Basic Data, 1982 (*Continued*)

| Country | Eligibility or Qualifying Conditions | Duration of Leave | Benefit Level or Rate | Financing | Job Security | Additional Benefits |
|---|---|---|---|---|---|---|
| Czechoslovakia | Natural mothers only. 270 days in insured employment during last 2 yrs. Eligibility continues for 6 mos after employment ceases. | 26 wks (35 for single mother), 4 to be taken before expected birth. 6 wks mandated after birth. | 90% of insured wage up to maximum. | Employer and government. | Same or comparable job guaranteed including seniority and pension rights. | Mother's allowance: for women giving birth to 2d and subsequent children, right to unpaid, job-protected leave from work until child is age 2, plus a flat-rate benefit. |
| Denmark | Natural and adoptive mothers. Employees and self-employed. Others may insure voluntarily. | 18 wks. 4 wks can be taken before expected birth; 14 wks after birth, or adoption (4 wks postchildbirth for nonearners). | 90% of weekly earnings up to maximum insured wage. | National government, 75%; local government, 25%. | Same or comparable job guaranteed; seniority, fringe benefits and pension rights protected. | For white-collar workers, benefit duration up to 5 mos including 2 mos before birth (if delay up to 3 mos) and a maximum of 3 mos after birth at a benefit level equal to 50% of wages. |
| Finland | Natural mothers and fathers. 3 mos in covered employment or in receipt of unemployment | 43 wks (10 mos), can be supplemented by annual vacation (at least 4 more wks), up to | 80% of average weekly earnings up to maximum insured wage. | Contributory: employer, 2% of wages; employee, 1.5%. | Same or comparable job guaranteed; seniority benefits and pension entitlements. | Supplementary 1 yr unpaid leave; can be used by either parent or shared. |

| | Eligibility | Duration of leave | Cash benefit | Financing | Job protection | Parental/other leave |
|---|---|---|---|---|---|---|
| | | insurance at that time. 8 wks can be taken before expected birth. Fathers may use up to 2 wks of postchildbirth leave. | | | | |
| France | Natural and adoptive mothers. 10 mos in covered employment; 200 hrs in first 3 mos of last 12 mos. | 16 wks including up to 6 wks before expected birth (2 wks required); and 10 wks after (6 wks required); 2 extra wks if multiple births or complicated delivery. 6 mos at birth of 3d or subsequent children. 10 wks for adopted child. | 90% of average insured earnings up to maximum insured wage. | Contributory: employer, 10.25% of wages up to specified amount, then 2%; employee, 2.5%, and then 1%. | Same or comparable job guaranteed; seniority and pension entitlements. | Parental Education Leave to care for a young child. Unpaid up to 2 yrs; can be used by father, too; contingent on certain type of work experience. |
| FRG | Natural mothers only. 12 wks (in covered employment) between 10th and 4th mo prior to confinement. | 7½ mos. 6 wks before expected birth (required) and 6 mos after birth. | Wage-related, to full net wage. From minimum of DM 3.5 per diem to maximum of DM 25 per diem. Additional supplementation, if wage level warrants it, by employer, for first 14 wks. | Contributory: employer and employee contributions. Government contributes DM 400 per beneficiary to health insurance fund, plus full payment for least 4 mos. | Same or comparable job guaranteed; seniority and pension entitlements. | — |

**Table 1.3.** Maternity and Parental Leaves—Basic Data, 1982 (*Continued*)

| Country | Eligibility or Qualifying Conditions | Duration of Leave | Benefit Level or Rate | Financing | Job Security | Additional Benefits |
|---|---|---|---|---|---|---|
| GDR | Natural mothers only. Employed women, full-time students and trainees. At least 6 mos employment during prior year or 10 mos in last 2 yrs. | 26 wks. 6 wks before birth (required) and 20 after. | Full net wage up to maximum insured wage. | Contributory: 10% from employer; 10% from employee. 20% from self-employed covers all social insurance benefits. | Same or comparable job guaranteed, including seniority and pension rights. | Supplementary Maternity Leave: 26 wks on the birth of a 2d and subsequent child paid at sickness insurance level (50% of wage with a minimum of EDM 300 per month). |
| Hungary | Natural mothers only. 9 mos employment in last 2 yrs.<br><br>6–8 mos employment qualifies for lower benefit. | 20 wks. Up to 4 wks before and 16 wks after confinement. | 100% of previous earnings up to maximum insured wage.<br><br>65% of earnings equals partial benefit. | Contributory: employer and employee. | Same or comparable job guaranteed, including seniority and pension rights. | Child Care Grant. Eligibility: 12 mos employment in last 18 mos or at least 90 days after full-time student status. Duration: up to child's 3d birthday. Benefit level: flat grant equal to about 40% of female wage. Job security: same as for maternity leave. |

| Country | Coverage | Duration | Benefit | Funding | Job protection | Supplementary |
|---|---|---|---|---|---|---|
| Israel | Natural and adoptive mothers. 10 mos in last 14, or 15 in last 22 mos in insured employment (if only 10 mos in last 18, get only half the benefit). | 12 wks, including 6 wks before childbirth. | 75% of average weekly earnings during last 3 mos, up to maximum insured wage. | Contributory: employer and employee contribute 0.4% of wage; self-employed contribute more. | Same or comparable job guaranteed, including seniority and pension rights. | Same entitlement for spouse of woman who died in childbirth or within 1 year of child's birth. |
| Italy | Natural mothers only. Currently working in covered employment. | 2 mos before childbirth (longer if birth is delayed) and 3 mos after. Mandatory leave. | 80% of wages up to maximum insured wage. | Contributory; but heavily weighted toward employer. | Same or comparable job guaranteed, including seniority and pension rights. | Optional supplementary 6 mos leave at 30% of average prior wage with full job protection. |
| Norway | Natural mothers and fathers. 6 mos insured employment during last 10 mos before expected delivery. Only mothers can use prenatal benefit. | 18 wks, including 6 wks before birth. 6 wks postchildbirth mandated for mother. Father can use up to 12 wks of total benefit. | 100% of average weekly wage up to maximum insured wage. | Contributory: employer; employee; national and local government. | Same or comparable job guaranteed, including seniority and pension rights. | Right to unpaid but job-protected leave for up to 1 yr; can be used by either parent or shared. |
| Poland | Natural mother only. Currently working in covered employment. | 16 wks for first child; 18 wks for second and subsequent. | 100% previous earnings. | 1.2–3% contributed by employee; 10–30% contributed by employer. (Varies by industry.) | Same or comparable job guaranteed, including seniority and pension rights. | Right to additional unpaid leave. |

**Table 1.3.** Maternity and Parental Leaves—Basic Data, 1982 (*Continued*)

| Country | Eligibility or Qualifying Conditions | Duration of Leave | Benefit Level or Rate | Financing | Job Security | Additional Benefits |
|---|---|---|---|---|---|---|
| Sweden | Natural or adoptive parent. Insured for 180 days for minimum cash benefit; worked in covered employment for 6 mos, for leave. Only mother can use prenatal leave. | 9 mos; up to 60 days before childbirth. Benefit can be prorated as portion of days. 3 mos more at minimum flat-rate daily benefit. | 90% of wage up to maximum insured wage. | Employer, 7% of wage up to maximum. Government pays 25% of costs. | Same or comparable job guaranteed, including seniority and pension rights. | Right to unpaid leave until child is 18 mos of age. Right to work 6-hr day (without extra compensation) until child is 8. |
| U.K. | Natural mothers only. Maternity allowance: at least 50 wks in covered employment. | M.A.: 18 wks, up to 11 wks before expected birth and 7 wks after. (Prenatal leave can be extended if birth is delayed.) | M.A.: flat rate, plus earnings related supplement if eligible, up to specified maximum. | Contributory. | Same or comparable job guaranteed, including seniority and pension rights. | — |
| | Maternity Pay: at least 2 yrs for same employer. | M.P.: 40 wks of leave. Up to 11 wks before and 29 wks after. | M.P.: 90% of wage for a maximum of 6 wks. | Contributory. | Full job protection. | — |

higher than the grant) for the first fourteen weeks of the seven-and-a-half month maternity leave.

In several countries employees in specified industries or specific companies may have supplementary coverage (full wage replacement over and above the insured wage, or a longer leave) as a consequence of labor-management agreements. Similarly, several countries provide additional benefits, or extended coverage, to public employees.

The benefit is universal; it is available to all otherwise eligible women regardless of income, in all countries. It is tax free in all countries except Sweden and Canada.

Except for Sweden, where a small minimum benefit is provided to any woman covered under health insurance, so that housewives may be covered, eligibility for these benefits is restricted to women who have been employed for at least some minimum time before childbirth.* Some countries now define adoptive mothers as eligible for the benefit as well as natural mothers. Coverage is extensive in almost all countries. In several, virtually all employed women who give birth are covered.

Sweden is the only country that provides this benefit to both parents, with fathers having approximately the same entitlement as mothers. Several other countries are debating extending their maternity leaves to cover fathers also. However, so far only Finland and Norway have actively moved in this direction and now give fathers the right to a portion of the overall maternity leave.

The benefit is very popular wherever it exists. In most countries there continues to be pressure to extend the duration of the benefit, to extend eligibility that would include adoptive mothers and fathers where they are not covered and to raise the benefit level to 100 percent of the maximum insured wage in those countries now providing less.

Although the specific benefit system may vary, in all countries the cash maternity benefit is one part of the social insurance or social security system. The benefits are financed in

---

* Australia provides a benefit for twelve weeks prior to childbirth and six weeks later to women regardless of labor force attachment. However, like most income maintenance programs in Australia, this one, too, is income tested.

whatever way social insurance is funded in the country, as either a contributory or a noncontributory benefit. Where it is a contributory benefit, it is usually the employer and the government who bear the burden, although in several countries (including Canada), the employee contributes directly.

While most countries provide these benefits through national health insurance, sixteen countries have such benefits despite the absence of health insurance. Various alternative policy instruments may be used to provide maternity benefits, including unemployment insurance (Canada and Austria); a special maternity benefit (Israel); parent insurance (Sweden); employment benefit (Britain); a combination of health insurance and mandated employer provision (Federal Republic of Germany).

All those countries that provide maternity leaves also provide medical and hospital coverage at childbirth as well as prenatal and postnatal care through a national health insurance system or national health service.

In recent years, several new benefits have emerged in a number of countries, adding a new and significant dimension to what was initially designed as protective legislation for women. At the same time, maternity leaves have been extended and benefit levels raised, suggesting that the initial function of these benefits has also been broadened. The new benefits include several variations on the right to an extended, job-protected leave from work with provision of a cash benefit, but usually at a lower level than for the basic maternity leave. Most of these countries also provide the right to extended, unpaid, but job-protected leaves for at least one year and often as long as two.

Even if the details and mode of provision vary, this international review of maternity policies should underscore how strangely unaccommodating American attitudes and commitments have been.

## WHY DO THEY DO IT?

An American reader will ask: Why the statutory provision elsewhere and not in the United States? Why do they have longer job-protected leaves, more generous and more extensive wage replacement? Don't Americans traditionally regard motherhood highly? Don't we value children and understand optimal conditions for child development in the early months of life?

The response can be either brief or lengthy. We have attempted a lengthy report elsewhere.[12] In brief:

— Many countries have a variety of health insurance that usually includes cash benefits for work days lost because of sickness. In such a context it is natural to specify wage replacement for a working woman home for childbirth. Related doctor and hospital costs are of course also met by the health insurance system.
— There are some countries with explicit family policies, which translate themselves into provisions for income support, maternity benefits, child care provision, housing, and health services—all geared toward family enhancement or support efforts.
— In some countries the trade or labor unions have defined maternity benefits as an important issue; in others one or another political party has.

## SUMMARY

Women are increasingly likely

— to be in the labor force during their prime childbearing years; 65 percent of 18 to 44-year-olds worked in 1980, and the rate is even higher among those under 35;
— to be in the labor force at the time of pregnancy and childbirth; 85 percent of working women are likely to become pregnant at some point in their working lives;
— to be in the labor force within one year after childbirth or considerably sooner, and those who work while pregnant are even more likely to have returned by then;
— to be making a significant contribution to family income if married, or to be the sole support if not. In the more than one quarter of all families in which women work full time all year round, they contribute an average of 39 percent of family income. In the age group 25 to 35, the peak childbearing years, over half of the women work full time all year.

Children are increasingly likely to be born into families in which their mothers are working (indeed may have worked until going into labor) and plan to return to work soon after childbirth. Yet there is growing evidence and strong opinion as to the importance of parent and child having some uninterrupted time together, especially in the early weeks, to cement their relationship and to launch the child's healthy development. Many authorities also emphasize the importance of similar opportunity for early and sustained maternal and paternal interaction with the child.

Finally, the experience in all other industrialized countries suggests the legitimacy of the widespread definition of maternity as a social risk, in the social insurance sense, like old age, disability, death of a survivor, unemployment. Women are making a contribution to the society when they have children, and the society in return undertakes to protect them against job loss and against temporary loss of income even as it protects the health of mother and child by ensuring that medical care will be available without cost to the mother.

It is surprising how little maternity policy is discussed publicly in the United States. The problem is not that there is no attention to the fact that women are working outside the home, but that there is preoccupation with matters other than maternity *benefits:* the possible negative effects on children caused by absence of working mothers from the home; the problems in arranging for satisfactory child care services; the implications for family income and for changed patterns of consumption, savings, and investment of the two-earner family; the alleged effects of maternal employment on family stress and family break-up; and the problems of ensuring workplace and salary equality for female workers. Policy makers, citizen groups, and some employers have joined researchers in exploring the ways in which women attempt to cope with the simultaneous pressures of work and family life. In doing so, they have looked at adult role changes, the consequences for the daily lives of children, and the likely permanence of these and related societal shifts.

Why in this context has maternity policy not received more sustained and widespread attention (we do not argue that it has been completely ignored)?

Perhaps because the growth in labor force participation rates of women with young children—especially married women—has been recent, or because the trend toward young women remaining in the labor force even after they give birth is not yet recognized, there has been little recognition of how many parents and children have a stake in maternity policy. Or perhaps the important point is that while a larger portion of young couples are eventually affected, those with a stake in this issue at any one time in any one workplace are limited in number and do not constitute a "critical mass" of visible social need. In any case, whatever the full explanation, there has been only limited systematic attention paid to how the workplace has responded or is responding to a female labor force increasingly likely to experience pregnancy and maternity at some point in its work history. That is the picture we will try to provide here. First we turn to a discussion of what the maternity policy is in the United States and how it evolved.

# 2. HISTORICAL NOTES ON MATERNITY POLICIES IN THE UNITED STATES

Another new college president, Ellen Futter of Barnard, gave herself a 32nd birthday gift yesterday—a 5-pound 9-ounce girl born at 1:30 A.M. at New York Hospital.

Miss Futter, who was appointed Barnard's president last May, and her husband, John Shutkin, decided to name the infant, their first child, Anne Victoria.

It was the first time a Barnard head had given birth to a child while holding office. In 1901, Emily Jane Smith Putnam informed the board of trustees she was pregnant, and was promptly dismissed.[1]

At the very core of the stereotypes which have resulted in irrational impediments to employment opportunity for women are assumptions about pregnancy—both its medical characteristics and physical effects, and, more broadly, assumptions about its implications for the role of women in society and in the labor force. Indeed, it is fair to say that most of the disadvantages imposed on women, in the work force and elsewhere, derive from this central reality of the capacity of women to become pregnant and the real and supposed implications of this reality.[2]

In considering the history of maternity policies we focus on four domains: (1) social-insurance related measures to protect income lost before or after childbirth; (2) measures to protect the health of the pregnant woman and of the mother, immediately before and after childbirth; (3) measures to protect women against job loss and related benefits at the time of pregnancy and childbirth; and (4) measures intended to facilitate the development of wholesome parent-child attachment.

Social insurance is considered to be societal protection against those risks viewed as beyond the control of the individual, or risks incurred while contributing to the well-being of the society as a whole. At the core of this perspective is concern with the protection of earned income when earnings are lost temporarily or permanently. Maternity benefits for employed women, as a social insurance benefit, are almost as old as sickness benefits, the oldest such benefit. They were established first by Bismarck in Germany about one hundred years ago. Before the onset of World War I, several European countries, including France, Italy, and Britain, had already legislated some form of national maternity insurance for working women. Moreover, in 1919, the International Labor Organization, at its first International Conference in Washington, D.C., produced the first international conventions on childbirth and maternity, as well as on children's employment and hours and shift work for women.

In actual practice, however, not all reforms dealing with working women were judged as actually benefiting them. In 1936, following a series of ad hoc studies, the International Labor Organization (ILO) began a systematic study of all aspects of women's work, reviewing the situation in all member countries. One issue was whether, in the guise of humanitarian concerns, protective policies were not really policies restricting women's employment and giving men priority in the labor market. As one writer comments, "One test of a government's intentions was how far it provided maintenance for women whom it prevented from working."[3] For example, if legislation required that women stop work six weeks (or two months) before anticipated childbirth, but provided no cash benefits to cover wages lost, the costs to women were clearly heavier than the benefits. Similarly, if pregnant women were not permitted to continue in physically demanding jobs yet employers were not required to provide alternative work at the same pay and no cash benefit was made available, they didn't really gain. On the other hand, some countries, including Italy and Japan in those years, extended maternity leaves and increased maternity benefits (allowances) at the same time.

Nonetheless, for all the inconsistencies of practice, by 1951 eighteen countries had ratified the 1919 Maternity Protection Convention of the ILO. The Convention and the 1952 revisions have had a major impact on the pattern of maternity protection throughout the world. The Convention called for a paid maternity leave of at least twelve weeks (a minimum of six weeks before and after childbirth), job protection during maternity leave (including protection of seniority and pension entitlements), full medical care or health insurance benefits, and nursing breaks during working hours. The United States has still not ratified that Convention.

Seventy-five countries, including all major industrial countries except the United States, now provide for maternity benefits through national legislation. Typically, such benefits initially emerged out of concern for the health of the mother; and the focus was on women as mothers, not women as workers. Where they existed, maternity benefit laws therefore provided for regular prenatal and postnatal physical examinations of the mother, excused periods from work at least twice daily to nurse infants, free health and medical care during pregnancy and at the time of delivery, and a paid leave for some time before and after childbirth. In the last ten to fifteen years, there has been a significant modification of these policies, however, moving from a primary focus on the woman worker and her physical health to a stress on the child and the needs of the child for nurturance, economic support, and physical care.

In contrast, until very recently almost no national policy in the United States has addressed the problem of working mothers, either from the perspective of their physical well-being, protection of their jobs, protection of income, or their children's well-being. No legislation yet assures women that their health and medical care expenses will be met at the time of maternity, or that they will be financially protected at that time, or that their infant will be assured of parental care, at least for a brief time after birth. Indeed, the maternal protection legislation that was written originally to protect future mothers at the workplace has often been used instead to reinforce women's isolation from the mainstream of productive labor and to constrain them from receiving equal benefits while working. This is only beginning to change.

## BACKGROUND AND ORIGINS OF MATERNITY POLICIES

The first statewide protective legislation for working women was passed in Wisconsin in 1867.[4] The movement to restrict the hours of employment for women (most generally to no more than ten hours per day and sixty hours per week) was based on the prevailing opinion, supported by medical testimony, that continuous standing, stretching, or repetitive motions weaken the childbearing abilities of young women and should therefore be limited. By the turn of the century sixteen states had laws restricting the hours of women's labor.

The first federal action regarding protective legislation for women was a landmark ruling of the Supreme Court in 1908.[5] Interestingly, a few years after rejecting protective labor laws for men, the Supreme Court in 1908 upheld similar legislation for women. In announcing this decision, the justices declared that because a woman is differentiated by physical structure, maternal function, and her dependency on men, "she is properly placed in a class by herself" for legislative purposes.[6] The court added that since healthy mothers are essential for healthy offspring, certain basic physical protection is essential for working women. Thus, for example, pregnant women should be excused from long working hours, especially if these involve much standing. As Judge Learned Hand stated in an opinion written in 1910:

It is known to all men . . . that women's physical structure and the performance of maternal functions place her at a great disadvantage in life; that while a man can work for more than 10 hours a day without injury to himself, a woman, especially when the burdens of motherhood are upon her, cannot.[7]

The authority of states to pass legislation limiting the hours of work for women as a class was confirmed. By 1912 thirty-four states had some legislation pertaining to hours of labor for women. Between 1910 and 1920 six states passed laws limiting the employment of women at the time they were due to give birth.[8]

## Married Women Should Not Work

At the same time, many, if not most, people viewed it unseemly and inappropriate for wives to work. An author writing about women workers in 1916 stated: "The American family standard has always been a bread-winning father, and a mother occupying herself with care of her children. Any deviation from this custom is cause for comment. Pride on the part of our native workmen serves to keep their wives out of the ranks of wage-earners."[9]

Samuel Gompers, the father of the American Federation of Labor and a supporter of equal pay for equal work, remained convinced that the place of married women, especially mothers, was in the home. Women participating in an American Institute of Banking Convention in 1923 were informed they were merely temporary employees, whose goal should be to return home. Pre-1930 "welfare capitalism" might provide company hospitals and company physicians to ensure good medical care for their female employees as well as the dependents of their male workers, but twentieth-century fringe benefits would be available far more sparingly to women workers at least until women workers were badly needed in the labor force once again. Given the employer's assumption that women were going to be marginal workers, there was no point in wasting benefits provided for the purpose of promoting loyalty and increased production on a population not expected to remain at work.

The idea that women belonged in the home to bear, rear, and care for children was pervasive in the 1920s and 1930s. Married women, who were thought to be taking jobs from men and single women, were described as being "a menace to the race . . . accountable for the falling birthrate, declining parental responsibility and decadence in home and family life."[10] Married women were often barred from employment altogether or dismissed when they got married. During the Depression, whole cities campaigned against working wives and most state legislatures considered bills to restrict the employment of married women. A National Education Association Study in 1930-31 revealed that 77 percent of all school systems surveyed refused to hire wives and 63 percent dismissed women teachers if they subsequently married. The belief that women should be home rearing children instead of working, or if working, should not be considered serious, permanent workers, made them a natural target when jobs were scarce. Most married women who continued to work despite marriage left work immediately when they became pregnant, knowing as they did that they would be discharged otherwise.

**Work When Needed: World War II**

If working wives were deemed unseemly in the 1920s and 1930s, World War II, with its accompanying work force shortage, made women workers essential to the war effort. As 4.5 million women entered the war labor force, a reassessment of employer policies and practices was essential.

To provide some nationwide guidelines for employers, the Women's Bureau in conjunction with the Children's Bureau issued "Standards for Maternity Care and Employment of Mothers in Industry" in July 1942. The standards noted that "a woman who is expecting a child should give first consideration to her own health and to plans for safeguarding the health and care of the child. Nevertheless, some women who are pregnant or who have young children may find it necessary to work."[11] Further, the standards recommended opportunity for prenatal care, a workday limited to eight daytime hours, rest periods, six weeks prenatal leave, two months postnatal leave, and restrictions in occupation or type of work, e.g., no lifting, continuous standing, or exposure to toxic substances. Maternity leave arrangements were recommended that would not jeopardize employment or seniority. The recommendation did *not* suggest a *paid* maternity leave.

The first federal legislation in the United States providing for maternity protection was passed in 1946 as an amendment to the Federal Railroad Unemployment Insurance Act. Under the act, pregnant women employees were entitled to temporary disability insurance and received weekly cash and sickness benefits for maternity. The program was financed by employees' contributions, a payroll tax, as were all other statutory benefits. At the inception of the program the maternity benefit duration was approximately sixteen and one-half weeks.[12]

A Children's Bureau study carried out in 1942 and 1943 took a hard look at employer practices affecting women, in particular the practice of firing women when they became pregnant or requiring them to take an unpaid leave of absence. The author of the study noted that while the reason often given for the practice was the protection of the mother and the fetus, and fear of liability for miscarriage, "aesthetic and moral" qualms were often at the root of such practices. Employers expressed the view that it was "not nice" for obviously pregnant women to be working in a factory and that it had a "bad effect" on male workers.[13] As late as 1974, the Supreme Court noted, in a footnote to a case challenging mandatory maternity "leaves" (unpaid, of course) in the fourth and fifth months of pregnancy, that the mandatory leave rule was inspired by the school district's desire to save pregnant teachers from embarrassment at the hands of giggling school children and to protect the children from the sight of conspicuously pregnant women.[14]

In fact, the practice of permitting a leave rather than outright discharge was a significant improvement over earlier practice and is said to have originated during World War II on the recommendations of the Department of Labor. Nonetheless, mandatory leave was also a vehicle for discrimination. It emerged as a major problem for working women and a target for elimination until accomplished in the 1970s.

**Work But Not When Pregnant: The 1950s and 1960s**

Women placed on mandatory unpaid leaves often found themselves little better off than when they were discharged. In the best of circumstances, a mandatory leave meant reinstatement in the same or a comparable job. Most of the time, however, such leaves were followed by reinstatement at a lower level job, with lower pay, or loss of benefits and seniority. For some women, returning to work after childbirth was the equivalent of beginning again, as if a new worker, regardless of the number of years on the job before. For many, loss of benefits meant loss of accrued entitlements to pensions, or it meant that at the time of childbirth, when it was especially important, they had no health insurance coverage or, if because of complications they became severely disabled, no disability coverage. Loss of seniority could mean loss of entitlements to vacation, to sick leave, and perhaps most important, to promotions and job opportunities.

The availability of mandatory leaves, without a series of guarantees of reinstatement at the same or a comparable level and without benefit and seniority protection, often was little more than a superficial gesture. Moreover, such a policy meant that women were often required to leave work well before they wanted to or thought they needed to. At the same time, postchildbirth job protection was almost nonexistent.

The first stirrings of official recognition of policy deficiencies began to emerge. In 1963, the President's Commission on the Status of Women made an extensive study of existing and needed protection for women workers. Maternity benefits were among the policies addressed.[15] In general, the Commission's conclusion was that, wherever practiced, legislation affecting labor standards should benefit men as well as women, especially where women employees might be placed at a disadvantage otherwise.

Two of the Commission's committees specifically considered the problem of maternity benefits for working women. The suggestion of the Committee on Social Insurance and Taxes was incorporated in the Commission's recommendation that "paid maternity leave or comparable insurance benefits should be provided for women workers; employers, unions, and government should explore the best means of accomplishing this purpose."[16] The Committee on Protective Labor Legislation suggested, further, that state legislation be enacted to ensure at least six months maternity leave without loss of reemployment and seniority rights. This is the first time such recommendations were made in a national, governmental report.

Both the elimination of mandatory leaves and the protection of job benefit and seniority while on leave became important legislative targets for many women in the 1960s and 1970s. Health protection, or the assurance of health and medical care, was not the issue, since national health insurance did not exist for anyone. Many male workers, not just women, were not covered under private insurance plans by their employers. (Even when women were covered, however, maternity coverage was often at a far lower level than medical coverage for other conditions requiring medical care or hospitalization.) The last major aborted effort at national health insurance had occurred almost two decades earlier, in the middle of World War II. A comprehensive social insurance plan was proposed, including, in addition to health insurance, a proposal for maternity benefits. The bill never came close to passing.[17] The National Health Insurance lobby would press forward in any case, but seemed unlikely to achieve success in the short term. National (federal) disability insurance under social security had only recently been legislated with much difficulty. Although coverage would be extended, it was still a long-term disability program and highly unlikely to grow beyond that.

Nor did efforts to respond to the maternity problem focus on unemployment insurance. Benefit levels have never been very generous, and the program didn't get much attention in the 1960s and 1970s except in the use of extended benefit coverage when the unemployment rate went up. Indeed, what relationship did exist between unemployment insurance and maternity protection took the reverse focus. In 1960, thirty-five states explicitly excluded pregnant women from eligibility for benefits, even if they qualified by all criteria; the period of exclusion ranged from between eight weeks and six months.[18]

Another vehicle took center stage in this battle. Legislation outlawing discrimination at work had existed since 1964 and provided a possible route for expanding rights and protections for women. The growing women's rights movement had begun to focus on issues of equity for women as individuals and workers, not women as wives and mothers.

Wendy Williams, an expert in this field, has commented as follows:

From the history, several things are apparent. One is that the common thread of justification running through most policies and practices that discriminated against women in the labor force rested ultimately on the capacity and fact of pregnancy and the roles, behavior patterns and mythologies surrounding it. Another is that because of pregnancy and motherhood, women were viewed as marginal workers not deserving of the emoluments and pay of "real" workers. The practices concerning pregnancy in particular arose not only out of the general attitudes described above but also out of a sense of embarrassment and discomfort at the presence of obviously pregnant women in the workplace.[19]

A reading of the literature surrounding the Supreme Court case to which Williams referred, or the testimony given at the hearings where she appeared, confirms this interpretation. The lack of protection at the time of pregnancy and maternity was viewed: (1) as a consequence of women's marginality to the labor force; (2) as a concomitant of the mystique surrounding pregnancy and a vestigial Victorian attitude suggesting that pregnancy was somehow "not nice" and should be hidden; and (3) as a problem of heavy costs, raising the fear that accompanied every effort at expanding social protection, whether the elimination of child labor, the enactment of social security, the establishment of a minimum wage, or negotiations for any additional fringe benefits.

## MATERNITY POLICIES AS SEX DISCRIMINATION

The most comprehensive and well-known law dealing with sex discrimination is Title VII of the Civil Rights Act of 1964, amended in 1972 and 1978. Title VII, outlawing all forms of employment discrimination based on race, color, religion, sex, or national origin, was the culmination of a twenty-year federal legislative effort to enact fair employment practice legislation. Specifically, Title VII provides that it is unlawful to discriminate with respect to "compensation, terms, conditions, or privileges of employment, because of sex."[20]

When Title VII became effective in 1965, only private sector employees working for employers with fifteen or more employees, were protected by its provisions. Congress amended the law in 1972 to include state and local government workers as well as federal workers, but the limitations on firm or organization size still remains.

Some states also have their own antidiscrimination laws. In several instances (New York, for example) these apply to firms with fewer than fifteen employees.

## Pregnancy Discrimination, Not Sex Discrimination

Although Title VII explicitly banned sex discrimination in all aspects of employment, there was no record concerning congressional intent as to whether childbirth and pregnancy-related disabilities were meant to be included. The question thus remained: is discrimination based on pregnancy a form of sex discrimination? Does the denial of benefits to pregnant employees, comparable to those given male and nonpregnant female employees, constitute sex discrimination?

Congressional silence on this point might be related to the fact that when the House Judiciary Committee reported out on the proposed legislation, sex was not mentioned as a protected classification.[21] Emanual Cellar, then chairman of that committee and a recognized civil rights advocate, stated that the Report of the President's Commission on the Status of Women had convinced him that "discrimination based on sex . . . involves problems sufficiently different from discrimination based on . . . other factors . . . to make separate treatment preferable."[22]

At the same time, Representative Howard Smith, an anti-civil rights advocate, offered an amendment to the proposed legislation. Hoping to kill the bill, he proposed that sex be included as another protected class under Title VII. The House accepted his amendment and went on to pass Title VII as did the Senate, with the sex classification intact.

In 1966, in response to a company's question as to whether excluding pregnancy and childbirth as a disability under a given plan would violate Title VII, the general counsel of the Equal Employment Opportunity Commission (EEOC) issued an opinion letter.

The Commission policy in this area does not seek to compare an employer's treatment of illness or injury with his treatment of maternity since maternity is a temporary disability unique to the female sex and more or less to be anticipated during the working life of most women employees. Therefore, it is our opinion that according to the facts stated . . . a company's group insurance program which covers hospital and medical expenses for the delivery of employee's children, but excludes from its long-term salary continuation program those disabilities which result from pregnancy and childbirth would not be in violation of Title VII.

Soon after, still another opinion letter was issued by the EEOC General Counsel, stating, "an insurance or other benefit plan may simply exclude maternity as a covered risk, as such an exclusion would not in our view be discriminatory." [23]

## A Changed Perspective: The 1970s

In 1972 the EEOC issued its "Guidelines on Discrimination Because of Sex," which reversed the earlier opinions. It provided, among other things, that disabilities resulting from "pregnancy, miscarriage, abortion, childbirth, and recovery therefrom are, for all job-related purposes, temporary disabilities" and must be treated as such under any health or temporary disability insurance or such leave plan that may be available to employees. One interpretation of this switch is that in amending Title VII in 1972, congressional debate had made more explicit and more central the significance of the legislative protections against sex discrimination. As a consequence, the new EEOC guidelines were issued to implement the intent of the Congress at that time.

Following the issuance of the "Guidelines," seven federal courts of appeals and eighteen federal district courts agreed that the EEOC guidelines reflected the intent of Congress and that to deny benefits available to other employees to pregnant women workers violated Title VII. Despite a spate of consistent rulings in 1975, the Supreme Court in 1976 held in *Gilbert* v. *General Electric Corporation* that the exclusion of pregnancy-related disabilities from a company's disability insurance program was not sex discrimination. [24] The majority decision concluded that men and women were covered under the G.E. plan for like risks except for pregnancy. No insurance plan had to include protection against all risks; and the fact that pregnancy was a risk affecting women only did not constitute discrimination.

Previously, the Supreme Court had rejected a challenge to the California State Disability Insurance Plan, which excluded normal pregnancies and childbirth from benefit coverage. Those challenging the California law argued that denial of benefits for a disability accompanying a normal pregnancy and childbirth was invidious discrimination based on sex and constituted a violation of the equal protection clause of the Fourteenth Amendment. The Court disagreed and rejected the challenge.[25]

The California Legislature nullified the Supreme Court decision in 1976 when it amended its disability legislation to cover normal pregnancies and childbirth for a total of six weeks. (See chapter 4 for some discussion of California policy.)

In the *Gilbert* decision, the Supreme Court, in effect, defined sex discrimination in the same terms as discrimination had traditionally been viewed under the Fourteenth Amendment. On that basis, excluding the condition of pregnancy from a temporary disability plan is not sex discrimination. One year later the Supreme Court ruled similarly in *Nashville Gas Co.* v. *Satty*[26] that the denial of sick pay to pregnant workers was not a violation of Title VII unless the employee who had brought the suit could offer evidence that the exclusion of pregnancy met the test the court had set down in *Gilbert:* the denial of sick pay to pregnant employees was a mere pretext purposely designed to discriminate against members of one sex or the other.

### Pregnancy and Maternity Discrimination As Sex Discrimination: The 1978 Legislation

The reaction to the *Gilbert* decision was immediate and intense. A coalition of women's organizations, civil rights organizations, and labor unions joined together in support of specific legislative reform. As a result, the effects of the Supreme Court decisions were undone in 1978 when the Pregnancy Disability Amendment to Title VII was passed (PL 95-555).

The amendment added subsection (k) to Section 701 of Title VII. The text follows:

(k) The terms "because of sex" or "on the basis of sex" include, but are not limited to, because of or on the basis of pregnancy, childbirth, or related medical conditions; and women affected by pregnancy, childbirth, or related medical conditions shall be treated the same for all employment-related purposes, including receipt of benefits under fringe benefit programs, as other persons not so affected but similar in their ability or inability to work, and nothing in section 703(h) of this title shall be interpreted to permit otherwise. This subsection shall not require an employer to pay for health insurance benefits for abortion, except where the life of the mother would be endangered if the fetus were carried to term, or except where medical complications have arisen from an abortion: *Provided*, That nothing herein shall preclude an employer from providing abortion benefits or otherwise affect bargaining agreements in regard to abortion.

In its first guidelines, the EEOC ruled (April 20, 1978) that (1) maternity benefits for wives of employees must be provided if husbands are covered under the company's medical plan, but a medical plan need not cover other dependents, and (2) disability or medical payment plans must begin providing the same benefits for pregnancy-related conditions as it provides for other conditions on or after April 29, 1979, even if the pregnancy began before that date.[27]

The amendment as interpreted now

1. expands the definition of sex discrimination to include discrimination based on "pregnancy, childbirth or related medical conditions";
2. requires employers to treat pregnancy and childbirth like other causes of disability under employee benefit plans such as health insurance, disability insurance, or sick leave plans. Except that an employer is not required to cover payment for an abortion unless the mother's life is endangered or medical complications occur as a result of an abortion;
3. prohibits mandatory leaves arbitrarily set at a specified time during a pregnancy and not based on the inability of the pregnant woman to work;
4. protects the reinstatement rights of women on leave for pregnancy-related reasons, including credit for previous service, accrued retirement benefits, and accumulated seniority; and
5. prohibits terminating a woman's employment, or refusing to hire or promote her, solely because she is pregnant.

The underlying principle of the amendment is that employment decisions concerning pregnant women must be based on their ability or inability to work, just as such decisions would be made about any other employee. Congress had made fully explicit that the fundamental aim of Title VII, to prohibit different treatment based on sex, included a prohibition against employment practices that deny pregnant women treatment equal to that given nonpregnant employees.

Although many companies had already begun to respond to the 1972 EEOC Guidelines, the 1978 legislation sharply accelerated the process among the laggard companies and offered confirmation of existing policy positions for the more advanced companies. The elimination of mandatory maternity leaves, the ending of refusals to hire pregnant women or firing them when they became pregnant, and the denial of seniority to women on leave have all become announced policy. Whether they have been implemented remains to be seen. Gross violations occur infrequently. More subtle discrimination continues (see chapter 5). Voluntary unpaid maternity leave continues to be permitted under Title VII, as long as made available in a nondiscriminatory manner.

## EQUAL TREATMENT: FOR THE PREGNANT AND THE NONPREGNANT

Equal treatment under group health insurance plans also became an intense issue at this time. Employee benefits plans are the most important source for health insurance protection in the United States. The Pregnancy Disability Legislation is designed to change hospital and maternity benefits plans that exclude coverage of pregnancy and childbirth, or plans that provide maternity coverage but less generous hospital and medical benefits than for other disabilities.[28] Employers are not required to have such a plan, but if it exists, these conditions must be covered in the same way as all other medical conditions.

As with health insurance, disability insurance and sick pay benefits are covered under the 1978 legislation, but employers are not required to provide them. Nor does entitlement to disability insurance or sick leave automatically follow from pregnancy. Employees must qualify for these benefits just as they would if disabled or ill for other reasons. Thus, medical (or, if authorized, religious) certification of inability to work may be required, and the benefit duration may be limited to a defined and certified period of incapacity, not to the maximum permitted under the plan.

The length of time a woman is disabled at the time of childbirth was an important issue during the hearings on the legislation and continues to be debated even after enactment of the law. Much of the concern expressed during the hearings had to do with the financial burden imposed on employers by requiring them to cover normal pregnancies and childbirth under sick leave and disability insurance, and the potential for abuse by women taking extended leaves, often with no intention of returning to work. The major concern was not the occasional pregnancy-related illness, nor even the 5 percent of pregnancies and childbirths that result in complications and more extensive hospitalizations or treatment. Most of the apprehension was directed rather at just how long before and after childbirth most women would stay out of work. Some expressed concern that women would view themselves as entitled to a nine-month paid leave. Others were sure that even if the prenatal leave were modest, women would expect to have six months post-childbirth leave.

Carol Bellamy, now New York City Council President, testifying as a New York state senator at the hearings in 1977, commented that business and industry feared that women would take the full twenty-six weeks allowable under New York State temporary disability law once normal pregnancies and delivery were covered.[29] She pointed out that although Hawaii does not monitor benefit periods by the type of disability, Prudential Insurance Company, a major writer of disability insurance in Hawaii, found that on the contrary, women took four weeks prior to childbirth and four weeks after delivery, but rarely more than eight weeks in toto.

A representative of the New York State Medical Society, testifying before the New York State Assembly Labor Committee in 1975, stated that while pregnancy disability is more subjective than many other disabilities, this should not be interpreted to mean that physicians and patients will collaborate to extend leave beyond an actual period of disablement. According to a representative of the society, the usual period of disability *after* birth is six to eight weeks. Thus, a disability claim of up to twelve weeks for a normal pregnancy would be reasonable. The New York State Division of Human Rights estimated that a six- to eight-week benefit period overall is "average" and "predictable." The New Jersey Commissioner of the Department of Labor and Industry stated that their figures indicated that an average claimant used 7.7 weeks. (See chapter 4 for some further discussion of the state experience.)

The discussion at the hearings concerning costs ranged widely. Representatives of the U.S. Chamber of Commerce, the American Council of Life Insurance, and the Health Insurance Association of America testified that the total costs of the legislation could be as high as $1.7 billion, representing about a 5.4 percent increase in the total cost of employee benefits, two-thirds of which would be attributable to health insurance costs. Others, including representatives of the U.S. Department of Labor and the AFL-CIO, took the position that no accurate cost estimates could be made since adequate data were not available. One problem, for example, had to do with what proportion of those covered under the "discriminatory" plans were female.

The range of costs estimated for extending disability insurance coverage was similarly wide. The Health Insurance Association of America estimated $571 million, the AFL-CIO $130 million, and the Department of Labor (DOL) $191.5 million. Only the DOL figures excluded workers already presumed to be covered; their estimate of average benefit duration was 7.5 weeks. The Health Insurance Association estimate assumed a far higher birthrate than any of the other estimates and a much longer benefit. The AFL-CIO estimate was based on the briefest benefit: six weeks.

## AN IMPLICIT NATIONAL MATERNITY POLICY

Even though all ramifications were not clear, by the close of the 1970s, a national maternity policy thus had been established—or perhaps more accurately, had been arrived at in a series of halting, somewhat circuitous steps. The policy was not the result of dramatic and coherent, specifically focused legislation, nor was it the expression of some clear societal consensus. Legislation relating to maternity largely rode the currents of other issues, particularly antidiscrimination, and often more directly addressed such other matters. Only in retrospect can accumulated aspects of administrative, legal, and legislative initiative be seen as creating implicit national maternity policy. In its main outlines, however, the nature of this policy, as well as its limitations, is quite clear.

Discrimination against pregnant women—or women at the time of childbirth—in hiring, firing, promotions, seniority, and employee benefits provision would be defined as sex discrimination and a violation of Title VII of the Civil Rights Act. Moreover, for purposes of income protection as well as health and medical protection, pregnancy and maternity would be defined as temporary disabilities. If companies carried disability plans, women would be guaranteed protection, as would any other temporarily disabled employee. Certainly, it would not be protection for the entire pregnancy, or for an extended postnatal period, but for whatever period of time a physician would view them as physically incapacitated and unable to work. Women had won a legal battle that could give them basic protection related to their own physical condition before and after childbirth. Neither the child's needs, nor motherhood, nor parenting was at issue.

What have been the results? What impact has there been on employment policies and practices in the private and in the public sectors, and on state and local policies? Which employers are providing benefits, and to whom? What proportion of women workers are in fact protected at the time of pregnancy and maternity and what are the characteristics of those who are not? What do these explicit provisions and implicit policies mean? For relevant data, we turn to the next chapter.

# 3. THE BENEFIT PICTURE: EMPLOYEE AND EMPLOYER PERSPECTIVES

There are three fundamental components of a maternity policy that are responsive to the needs of families with children. Additional elements may be important and will enrich the policy, but unless these three are present as a minimum, the policy cannot be adequate. The three basic components are:

— *health insurance*, covering hospitalization and physician care for the mother and infant, including prenatal and postnatal care, as well as care at the time of childbirth;
— *a job-protected leave* for a specified period of time with protection of seniority, pension, and other benefit entitlements, and with assurance of the same or a comparable job on return to work;
— *full or partial wage replacement* (or salary continuation) through an insurance plan or on some other basis to cover all or a significant portion of the job-protected leave.

Our review of maternity policies throughout the world clearly indicates that an international consensus, represented in programmatic commitments, supports this view. As will be evident, the United States still falls far short of this standard.

## HEALTH INSURANCE COVERAGE

STATISTIC OF THE WEEK
Congratulations! It's a ($2,300) boy: the medical cost of having a baby climbed to $2,307 last year, according to a periodic survey of 200 hospitals by the Health Insurance Association of America. Almost two-

thirds of that ($1,450) goes for the hospital stay, including an average three days in a semiprivate room, as well as labor and delivery-room charges. Other charges include the services of the attending obstetrician ($642) and anesthesiologist ($150) and the pediatrician's newborn care ($64). If the delivery is by caesarean section—as it is in nearly one in every five births—the average cost goes up by more than 50 per cent, to $3,554. In 1978, the last time the association's survey was conducted, it cost $1,456 to have the same baby. (*National Journal* 1/8/83)

Clearly, having a baby is expensive! How do working parents manage?

The best available evidence indicates that about three-quarters of all full-time workers have basic medical insurance coverage through their employer, usually hospitalization and surgical coverage.[1] More specifically, this coverage is extended to 83 percent of full-time public employees, and 73 percent of all private wage and salary workers. However, these highly aggregated figures, relating to both men and women workers, conceal gaps in coverage that must be recognized in evaluating present provisions for maternity.

Most important, one-third of all women working in the private sector, including almost 30 percent of the divorced and separated women, do not have basic medical coverage. However, some married women who do not have coverage in their own right are covered as dependents under their husband's entitlements. Young adults aged 19 to 24, regardless of sex and labor force status, are twice as likely to be uncovered as older workers.[2] Part-time workers fare even worse: only 15 percent had such coverage in 1979. We draw attention to their low level of coverage because women constitute more than one-half (56 percent) of the part-time labor force, and about one-third of all working women worked part time in 1979.

The *1977 Quality of Employment Survey* (QES), a large, nationally representative sample of all workers who worked at least twenty hours a week, provides another perspective on the gaps in coverage. About one-quarter of married women who make such a commitment to paid labor are not covered by a health insurance plan. For single mothers, coverage was not extended to a third.

Together, these data point to a particularly acute problem among young and single mothers in the labor force, mothers who are relatively likely to lack coverage in their own right as workers or as a dependent of a spouse. Unfortunately, we lack the data necessary to estimate the extent of *family* coverage (whereby a husband's insurance covers his wife's birth-related costs). We also lack systematic information on the extent of coverage for maternity among those who are covered by some kind of health insurance. However, the gaps in health insurance coverage appear concentrated among women in prime child-bearing years.[3]

Of course, these gaps reflect the fact that not all private employers offer coverage to employees. In our own 1981 survey (discussed later), 95 percent of the responding companies stated that they provided such insurance benefits for their female employees; however, of these, only 84 percent offered full coverage. Maternity coverage seems to be somewhat less available to workers at the smallest firms, though 87 percent of the responding firms with fewer than twenty-five employees said they make such provision. Since our survey was least successful in tapping these very small companies, we assume our figures are overly generous. Indeed, the Health Insurance Institute 1980 survey, "New Group Health Insurance Policies Issues in 1980," found that only 76 percent of the smallest companies provided maternity coverage, and of these, only 79 percent extended a full plan. Since women are far more likely than men to work in small firms, this means they are even more likely to be at risk of no health insurance coverage for maternity. More comprehensive medical insurance covering routine physician (or pediatrician) visits and prescriptions are, of course, much less available.

Thus, for this first basic component of a responsive maternity policy, we find that a significant proportion of women is inadequately provided for. To be sure, most working women are insured against the medical costs of pregnancy and childbirth, either in their own right or as wives. Yet in relying on private initiatives for the provision of health insurance, our society in effect accepts the fact that significant numbers of families will have to bear these costs themselves and a sizable number will have no such coverage. We are unable to specify the dimensions of this gap in coverage because of inadequate data on the extent to which women not covered are included within their husbands' plans, but for the rapidly increasing numbers of single mothers such concerns for family coverage are entirely irrelevant. If pressed, we would very roughly estimate that some 10 percent of all employed women (those working in the public and private sectors) in prime childbearing years lack any health insurance coverage, through private insurance, Medicaid, or CHAMPUS (Civilian Health Insurance for the Military and Veterans), in their own right or as dependents, and that a still higher percentage may be uncovered among the nonworking. (See tables 3.1 and 3.2 for data on employed women.) During periods of high unemployment, as when we went to press in 1983, the proportions without any coverage rise substantially.

## JOB-PROTECTED MATERNITY LEAVE

A major development of the 1970s is that a leave at the time of childbirth, albeit a brief one, became available to most workers. Generally, during this leave, a woman's seniority and pension rights are protected, and she receives some assurance of

**Table 3.1.** Women Without Any Type of Health Insurance, by Employment Status (1977)

| Employment Status of Women (in 1,000s) | Number and Percent with No Health Insurance | |
|---|---|---|
| Worked full-time all year 20,972 | 1,875 | 8.9% |
| Worked at some time 8,726 | 959 | 11.0% |
| Never worked 11,191 | 1,071 | 9.6% |
| Unknown 518 | 63 | 12.0% |
| Total 41,407 | 3,968 | 9.6% |

SOURCE: National Center for Health Services Research, National Medical Care Expenditure Study, special analysis prepared for this study.

**Table 3.2.** Type of Health Insurance Coverage of Employed Women, by Employment Status (1977) (numbers in thousands)

| Employment Status | Private Health Insurance always, with and without other insurance | Private Health Insurance sometimes, without other coverage | Private Health Insurance sometimes, with CHAMPUS | Private Health Insurance sometimes, with Medicaid | CHAMPUS only[a] | Medicaid only | CHAMPUS and Medicaid | No Health Insurance | |
|---|---|---|---|---|---|---|---|---|---|
| Worked full-time all year 20,972 | 16,295 (77.7%) | 1,540 (7.3%) | 53 (.2%) | 114 (.5%) | 396 (1.9%) | 652 (3.0%) | 32 (.1%) | 1,875 (8.9%) | 20,957 (99.6%) |
| Worked some time 8,726 | 5,787 (66.3%) | 776 (8.9%) | 9 (1.0%) | 175 (2.0%) | 246 (2.8%) | 738 (8.5%) | 26 (.3%) | 959 (11.0%) | 8,716 (100.8%) |
| Never worked 11,191 | 7,323 (65.4%) | 490 (4.4%) | 21 (.2%) | 72 (.6%) | 263 (2.4%) | 1,916 (17.0%) | 28 (.2%) | 1,071 (9.6%) | 11,184 (99.8%) |
| Unknown 519 | 398 (77.0%) | 10 (2.0%) | — | 7 (1.0%) | — | 31 (6.0%) | — | 63 (12.0%) | 509 (98.0%) |

SOURCE: National Center for Health Services Research, National Medical Care Expenditure Study, Special Analysis. Prepared for this study.
[a] Civilian Health and Medical Program of the Uniformed Services (CHAMPUS) and Civilian Health and Medical Program of the Veterans Administrations (CHAMPVA).

having the same or comparable job on her return to work. At the same time, virtually all companies have eliminated the imposition of fixed limits on how long a woman may work during her pregnancy. (Many employers do require certification from the employee's own physician that it is safe for her to continue working.) The 1970s was a period, then, in which companies were willing to make some limited commitments to women employees but not, as will be detailed, to protect them against loss of income. For a large majority, the birth of a child does not now necessarily mean a choice between that child and a job, though the overwhelming number still have to forego all earnings during part or all of that leave. For a single mother, or a woman married to a man earning a low wage, the financial consequences obviously could be severe, for herself and for her child.

Even if a job-protected leave alone still falls far short of a responsive maternity policy, we will see that it represents a notable development in comparison to the very recent past. Yet, as also will be clear, our discussion of the extent and distribution of various benefits and policies must be somewhat tentative, relying as it does on imperfect employee- and employer-based data.

## The Quality of Employment Survey (QES)

The most representative general picture given by employees of the availability of benefits in the late 1970s is provided by *The 1977 Quality of Employment Survey.*[4] Overall, of the women working at least twenty hours per week in 1977, 75 percent of the respondents said they were entitled to some job-protected leave, a 12 percent increase since 1969.

Like many other employee benefits, eligibility for maternity leave with reemployment rights varies by the size of the company (see table 3.3). Women employees of large firms (500+ employees) are clearly most likely (89 percent) to have a guaranteed job if they take maternity leave, and indeed the likelihood of such a guarantee increases directly with firm size. At the very smallest firm (1–9 employees), the worksite for 14 percent of the women respondents to QES, only 39 percent claim to have this guarantee.

**Table 3.3.** Maternity Policies, by Establishment Size

| Number of Employees at Work Site | Percentage Eligible for Maternity Leave with Reemployment Rights* | | Percentage Eligible for Maternity Leave with Pay* | |
|---|---|---|---|---|
| 1–9 employees | 39% | (22) | 10% | (6) |
| 10–49 employees | 71% | (98) | 18% | (25) |
| 50–499 employees | 80% | (96) | 37% | (44) |
| 500 or more employees | 89% | (84) | 47% | (42) |
| Total | 74% | (300) | 29% | (117) |

SOURCE: 1977 Quality of Employment Survey.

*Percentages computed on a base of those definitely claiming coverage or not; all responding "don't know" are excluded.

## The Conference Board Data

A much more optimistic picture emerges from a widely noted Conference Board study of corporate policies relating to maternity. On the basis of their 1978 survey, the Conference Board reported that 97 percent of the companies in their sample allowed their female employees a job-protected leave immediately before and after childbirth.[5] Their conclusion was that such a policy is "virtually universal now."

Like other Conference Board surveys, however, this study is heavily weighted toward the practices of larger corporations and accordingly cannot be used for projections about all sectors of the economy. Moreover, the 1978 legislation should have had a significant impact on the extensiveness of these benefits. The findings of this study therefore seem most useful for considering the similarities and variations in the maternity policies of companies in what may be loosely called the large corporate sector at the end of the decade, just prior to the implementation of this legislation.

This 1978 study indicates that almost all corporations have eliminated a fixed time limit on pregnant women's right to continue working, that is, as long as they are healthy and able to do their work. Most companies also do not set restrictions on when in the pregnancy the maternity leave may start. This policy clearly reflects the impact of the Equal Employment Opportunity Commission's 1972 "Guidelines on Discrimination Because of Sex." These guidelines mandate that "the commencement and duration" of maternity leave as well as the "availability of extensions" must be in accord with the "same terms and conditions" that apply to leaves due to other temporary disabilities.[6] Their effect on corporate policies relating to maternity leave was dramatic. In 1964, about three-quarters of the manufacturing firms in a Conference Board survey had specified the point at which pregnant employees could no longer work—usually three to six months after conception!

These larger corporations also appear remarkably willing to grant maternity leaves to new employees. Less than half report a service requirement, and about another quarter require three months or less employment. However, corporations are less consistent in allowing sick pay for absence days resulting from pregnancy: about two-thirds make these payments.

By contrast, there is hardly a corporate consensus on what the length of leave should be. Somewhat less than half of the companies reporting a maximum leave grant four to six months of time off; approximately one-quarter offer extremely limited leaves of three months or less; and about an equal number grant more than a half year, though rarely more than a year. (Extensions are generally granted on a physician's certification of continued disability.) These maximums usually apply to the length of the entire leave (which may be started during pregnancy), but some only limit the time of leave after delivery.

We thus have a fairly good sense of leave policies within the corporate sector, the relatively progressive vanguard, but to get a picture of policies within the private sector as a whole, it is necessary to consider a wider range of companies.

## Maternity Benefits in the Private Sector: 1981 (The Columbia University Study)

The purpose of our own small-scale study was to provide an exploratory perspective on private sector maternity benefits and leaves in 1980–81. Since there was little systematic knowledge about these policies, the design of the study was premised on the view that the most sensible approach was to develop a preliminary awareness of how the corporate welfare system treats maternity and to identify pressing issues for further, more detailed analysis. In particular, we were interested in assessing the impact of the 1978 legislation and updating as well as improving earlier pictures of benefit coverage.

In line with this aim, the study was designed to delineate some of the main features of corporate maternity policy and also to suggest how policies vary by industry, company size, and certain work characteristics. The results of this study cannot be considered definitive. A much larger research effort, involving a substantially larger sample, is necessary for any such claims. The small scale of our research necessitates that findings must be considered provisional. Nevertheless, the sample includes a wider range of firms than any previous study covered.

For this effort to be valuable, it seemed essential to gather information on policies in a wide range of companies, from the largest corporate enterprises to local trade and service establishments. Our previous review of corporate benefits policies strongly indicates that larger firms have much more substantial benefits than smaller firms and that provision of benefits varies by industry as well.[7] Reanalysis of the QES also indicated that this pattern held for maternity-related policies. Our study was designed, then, to complement existing studies that focus almost exclusively on the practices of large corporations and therefore cannot be used for projections about practices in the great number of medium and small-sized firms. In a partial replication of the 1978 Conference Board study, we posed many of the same questions concerning maternity policies to a broader sample.

For technical details on the sample, we refer readers to the appendix. Here we may simply note that our analysis is based on responses from 250 companies. These companies may be seen as broadly representative of American companies with at least modest net worth (in excess of $500,000), though it is important to stress that our sample excludes very small firms and probably underrepresents the smaller firms which did qualify for inclusion in the sample. For these reasons, *our analysis is likely to overstate the benefits provided by American business.*\*

## FINDINGS

Much in line with the Conference Board's findings, 97 percent of the firms responding stated that employees are permitted to work right up to the time of delivery, if healthy and able to do the work. Less than half of the employers (46 percent) require their workers to bring in a certificate from their physicians certifying this. Instead, employers seem as likely to require a physician's statement certifying the inability of an employee to work, as the employee's ability to work. Indeed, except where the work is physically demanding, the policy of most employers seems to be that the decision regarding whether and when to leave work during pregnancy should be completely up to the employee.

Concerning a maternity leave, 88 percent of employers in our survey indicated that such leaves are provided. However, only 72 percent stated that they formally guarantee employees on maternity leave the same or a comparable job and assure them protection of seniority. We assume that the policy is informal and probably discretionary in most of the firms permitting such a leave but not providing a formal guarantee of job protection. Considering that many companies do not actually guarantee job protection, the policy of a protected leave is not "virtually universal" *throughout all sectors of the economy,* even if it is within large corporate business.

Most companies that provide a job-protected leave instituted such policies in the 1970s. Fewer than a quarter of the respondents stated that they had such a policy in 1969. By 1978, the number had almost tripled, and within two years after the passage of the 1978 legislation, another quarter of the companies had established such a policy.

\*The reader should know that all figures in the text and tables which are based on the Columbia University Study reflect the aggregated results of the telephone and mail survey if the items were included on both surveys (see appendix). Also, the number of cases in the tables varies because of missing data.

Firms in the retail trade and service industries are the least likely to provide leaves, or if permitting a leave, to guarantee the job on return. In contrast, banks and financial and insurance companies are the most generous. The size of the company is important, too, and may be even more so than the type of industry. Firms with fewer than twenty-five employees are particularly unlikely to permit a leave, or if permitting it, not to guarantee the job; firms with between twenty-six and ninety-nine employees are not much more generous.

Policies vary, as well, with regard to when the leave can begin, how long it can last, and what qualifies an employee for such a leave. Almost half of the respondents support a flexible policy in which the commencement of the leave depends on the woman, her particular job, her medical condition, and her own preference. Their policy, therefore, is to individualize the decision based on a variety of factors rather than to specify a particular time. Among those employers specifying a time, four to six weeks before expected childbirth is most typical. About a quarter of the respondents said that this was their policy.

Few employers (of those who grant a leave) permit more than a six-month maternity leave overall; considerably more than half limit the leave to three months or less (see table 3.4). Two or three months is the most common policy; almost 60 percent of the firms granting some leave indicate that this is their policy (28 percent allow three months and 33 percent two). In addition, over 10 percent have a discretionary policy whereby the maximum leave granted varies, just as the beginning date of the leave varies. (In practice, this seems to usually mean two months for a normal pregnancy and delivery.) About 20 percent of the responding companies with some provision for leave allowed a four- to six-month leave, while about 8 percent permitted more than this.

These findings on the maximum length of a job-protected leave strongly suggest that previous estimates, based on Conference Board data or other surveys of the large corporate sector, have overstated the generosity of leave policies within the private sector as a whole and are likely to exaggerate how extensive a leave is actually available to working mothers.

**Table 3.4.** Maximum Length of Leave, by Number of Employees

Companies Granting Some Leave

| Maximum Leave | Number of Employees | | | | |
| --- | --- | --- | --- | --- | --- |
| | *1–25* | *26–99* | *100–499* | *500+* | *Total* |
| 2 months or less | 41% | 37% | 33% | 17% | 33% |
| 3 months | 28% | 24% | 29% | 31% | 28% |
| 4–6 months | 7% | 23% | 21% | 17% | 19% |
| 7+ months | 7% | 6% | 4% | 21% | 8% |
| Varies | 17% | 10% | 14% | 14% | 12% |
| | 100% | 100% | 100% | 100% | 100% |
| | (29) | (63) | (55) | (30) | (177) |

Companies with Specified Length of Leave

| | *1–25* | *26–99* | *100–499* | *500+* | *Total* |
| --- | --- | --- | --- | --- | --- |
| 2 months or less | 50% | 40% | 38% | 19% | 38% |
| 3 months | 33% | 26% | 34% | 37% | 31% |
| 4–6 months | 8% | 26% | 24% | 22% | 22% |
| 7+ months | 8% | 7% | 4% | 22% | 9% |
| | 100% | 100% | 100% | 100% | 100% |
| | (24) | (58) | (49) | (26) | (157) |

SOURCE: Columbia University Study.
NOTE: All percentages are rounded.

As we stressed, our study is too small to provide firm estimates, but the discrepancy between our findings and those of the Conference Board is large, and any bias within our own response group is also likely to lead to some overstatement, not understatement, in the generosity of provisions in the private sector.

Furthermore, breakdown of leave policies by firm size within our sample at least tentatively suggests that the practices of large business are hardly typical (see table 3.4). Plainly, we have too few cases to specify the relationship between firm size and leave policies, but it appears that smaller firms are relatively likely to offer short leaves. The difference between the practices of the largest firms in our sample (500+ employees) and the smallest (1–25 employees) seems particularly pronounced.

Of course, the discrepancy between our data and earlier surveys—or at least some of it—may indicate that companies have reduced the maximum leave provided earlier, not that our findings are more representative. However, responses to our survey suggest that a significant proportion of companies only instituted such policies after 1978; therefore, a trend to shorter leaves seems unlikely. It is also possible that, in the late 1970s, only leading (and large) firms provided for such leaves, and they were relatively generous. As the policy has been extended across a wider range of employers, especially among more small and medium-sized companies, a more time-limited policy may have come to prevail (see chapter 5). Whatever the case, it seems that leave policies are now generally much less generous than commonly supposed.

We might add that a 1980–81 survey of two-career families found that the actual behavior of employees followed a pattern that resembled the maximum leaves reported in our study: 37 percent of the career women took time off for less than eight weeks after childbirth, and another 32 percent were on leave for nine to eighteen weeks.[8] Thus, more than two-thirds of the women were back at work less than four months after giving birth, and most took off no or little time before birth. Whether such relatively short leave reflected choice or company restrictions, though, is impossible to say.

A discrepancy between the Conference Board findings and our own also emerges when we look at the criteria established to qualify a woman for a leave. The Conference Board's study suggested that more than half of the firms permitting a leave had no minimum service requirement. By contrast, an overwhelming majority of our respondents (84 percent) have such a requirement (table 3.5): 28 percent require that an employee has worked for the firm at least one year before being eligible for such a leave, 15 percent require at least six months work, and 20 percent define three months as a minimum. Once again, whether these data reflect the inclusion of more smaller companies in our sample or changes in policy is difficult to discern, but at present a considerable service requirement is frequently imposed.

**Table 3.5.** Minimum Employment to Be Eligible for Leave

| Service Requirement | Columbia University Study (1980–81) | |
|---|---|---|
| | All Responses | Of Those with Service Requirements |
| None | 16% | — |
| 1–2 months | 6% | 8% |
| 3 months | 20% | 28% |
| 4–6 months | 14% | 20% |
| 9–22 months | 32% | 44% |
| 36 months | * | 1% |
| Varies | 12% | — |
| | 100% | 101% |
| | (145) | (105) |

| Service Requirement | Conference Board Survey (1978) |
|---|---|
| None | 57% |
| 1–2 months | 6% |
| 3 months | 13% |
| 4–6 months | 10% |
| 7–12 months | 13% |
| More | — |
| | 99% |
| | (127) |

NOTE: The Conference Board survey has no "varies"; larger companies are likely to have standard policies, it seems.

*Under 1 percent.

For most employees, the availability of a job-protected maternity leave means not only that they need not fear job loss if they take time off for childbirth, but, almost as important, that their health and medical insurance, as well as other benefits, are protected while they are on leave. An overwhelming number of the respondents stated that pension and life insurance benefits are continued for employees during their maternity leave either on a contributory or noncontributory basis (see table 3.6). As to health insurance, more than half of the respondents indicated that the employee continues to be protected without any contribution on her part, while about 40 percent stated that continu-

**Table 3.6.** Continuity of Benefits During Leave Among Companies
Providing Benefits Prior to Pregnancy/Maternity

|  | Life Insurance | Pension | Health Employee | Health Dependent(s) |
|---|---|---|---|---|
| Benefit not continued | 3% | 7% | 1% | 1% |
| Benefit continued with employee contribution | 35% | 15% | 44% | 65% |
| Benefit continued with no contribution | 62% | 78% | 55% | 34% |
|  | 100% | 100% | 100% | 100% |
|  | (156) | (124) | (157) | (147) |

SOURCE: Columbia University Study. These data suggest the percentage of companies with a benefit (prematernity leave) that discontinues coverage during leave; companies without the benefit are excluded.

ity of participation depended on the employee's contribution. Although two-thirds of the respondents stated that dependent coverage while an employee was on maternity leave was contingent on the employee's contribution, our data do not allow us to determine whether this greater emphasis on employee contribution is a consequence of a changed status (pregnancy and maternity) or continues the usual pattern.

The right to a leave at the time of childbirth has largely, but far from universally, been won by female workers. That this is an important right cannot be denied. After all, for years, women were discharged as soon as they were visibly pregnant. And if not discharged immediately, they were required to leave not too far along in their pregnancy. Now the decision to leave is made by the individual employee in conjunction with her doctor. When her doctor states she should stop work, she is entitled to do so. Many women elect to stop work some weeks before anticipated birth; some work up to the last moment. Their preference, however, prevails.

Most employers will hold a woman's job open at least for a minimally reasonable period after childbirth and at least assure her of a comparable job, if not the same one, on her return. We would emphasize here that for most employers this does not present a significant problem. Almost one-third of the respondents to our survey indicated that none of their employees was on maternity leave in 1979, and more than one-third said only one or two employees were out that year.

If the right to a leave is no longer in question for most working women, important aspects of this right are still at issue. Among these are when the leave ends, the length of the leave, the definition of a comparable job, and the nature of benefit protection, as well as the woman's rights while on leave. We will return to these aspects later.

### Fathers and Adoptive Parents

In discussing maternity benefits, we do not mean to slight the accommodations that may be made for fathers wanting to take on child care responsibilities, nor the possible importance of such policies. It is a measure of prevailing sex role norms and corporate policy that only a few advocates mention paternity leave. No reliable data exist as to their availability as an employee benefit. A very few companies, such as IBM, AT&T, and Equitable Life Assurance permit such leaves. One recent survey of companies in the large corporate sector found that 9 percent of the firms provide such leaves, though the details of these policies are unclear.[9] A quarter of the firms in our survey reported that they permit fathers time off, but this initially startling figure does not indicate much commitment to the parental responsibilities of fathers. For most, these policies mean a few days maximum, usually as part of sick leave. Only a few of the companies suggested that more generous accommodations might be arranged, and among those, when we explored further, the usual response was that even if there was the possibility of some informal "policy," few fathers inquired about it and still fewer took advantage of it.

Similarly, all of what we have discussed applies to natural parents only. Although a 1980 report indicates that fourteen companies provide adoption benefits (nineteen by 1981), not only is this coverage available just to a minute proportion of the labor force, but the benefit relates only to adoption costs, not to paid leave at that time.[10]

## PAID LEAVES—WAGE REPLACEMENT OR SALARY CONTINUATION: THE 1970s

Although the right to a leave from work at the time of childbirth, with full protection, offers some help to women, few can afford to take more than a very brief leave unless they and their families are protected against loss of income. Unfortunately, the provision of pay during maternity leave seems to be far from prevailing practice.

Thus, the third component of the maternity benefit package clearly remains the least adequate: the income benefit, be it through disability insurance, or sickness benefits, or some other form of salary continuation. Not only is coverage inadequate, but benefit levels are often low, the duration of the benefit period is brief, benefits are inconsistently provided by companies, policies are often confusing, and confused employees are sometimes, as a consequence, resentful. Furthermore, the data necessary to detail this indictment are woefully inadequate.

To the extent that paid maternity leaves exist in the United States, they do so largely as part of the employee benefits system. The Pregnancy Discrimination Act of 1978 requires that pregnant employees be treated the same as employees with any other temporary disability. This presumably means that women employed in firms with fifteen or more employees and providing short-term sickness or disability insurance have paid maternity leaves. However, the fact that the new law prohibits discrimination based on pregnancy is no guarantee that women employees are actually eligible for pregnancy or maternity benefits, or, indeed, that eligible employees are granted the benefits to which they are entitled. How this legislation has actually affected working women at the time of maternity is not yet clear. Among other matters, there is still controversy on how to comply with the law. Policy implementation is still in process.

We begin by providing data from the QES, giving the most

recent picture from the perspective of the employee. We continue with the findings from the Conference Board survey and then, from our own survey, the most recent available picture, even if necessarily crude, of what employers provide today.

## The Quality of Employment Survey

Twenty-nine percent of the QES respondents—all working at least twenty hours per week—stated that they were eligible for a maternity leave with pay, twice those eligible at the end of the 1960s. The availability of this benefit to workers varies by economic sector, much as the generally more common unpaid leave. Thus employees in small firms are far less eligible than those in large firms. Close to half of the employees in firms with more than 500 workers are entitled to such a benefit as compared with less than 10 percent in firms with fewer than 10 employees and 18 percent in firms with 10 to 49 employees. (See table 3.3.)

When we compare coverage for women working in different industries, the picture is again similar to that for unpaid leave. Coverage for maternity benefits in the wholesale and retail trade and nonprofessional service industries is particularly low; but with the slight exception of the financial and insurance firms, no major industrial groups stand out as particularly ahead. The laggard status of the trade and service industries appears to reflect in large part the generally small size of the firms within these industries. Female employees of small firms within other industries are much less likely to be granted maternity benefits than those in the larger firms. Indeed, among the employees of small firms (fewer than fifty employees), there is relatively little variation by major industrial category.

As a related note, it is striking that so many women employees—about a sixth—do not know if they have maternity leave with reemployment or with pay. (In comparison, almost all respondents made a definite statement on whether they had medical insurance.) Thus, assuming that the positive claims for coverage are accurate, actual eligibility may be somewhat more widespread than reported here. Of course, maternity benefits are not salient to all women employees in the same way health insurance is likely to be—hence the lower level of awareness. It is notable, though, that the proportion of "don't know's" is generally higher among the employees of smaller firms. Since employees of smaller firms are not unaware of their coverage on other benefits, this pattern of response may suggest that many smaller companies simply do not have clearly formulated maternity policies. Informal ad hoc arrangements may be particularly prevalent within smaller firms, and women employees may therefore be uncertain of what is available to them.

**The Conference Board**

Some 40 percent of the companies in the Conference Board 1978 study reported that they paid mothers while on maternity leave—about half through a noninsurance sick-pay plan, another half through a short-term disability insurance plan, or a combination of the two. The level of coverage suggested by this employer-based survey is again clearly much higher than that reported by the QES.

Generally, at the large firms included within this sample, the insured plans limit the duration of the benefit payments to six weeks, and limit the benefit level either to a low maximum or to a relatively low proportion of weekly wage. The uninsured plans do not set special limits on duration of leave, usually paying full salary for as long as a doctor certifies disability within the limits applicable to other benefits. Crucial is length of service; the median allowable period of benefit payments for a one-year employee is two weeks; for a five-year employee, it is nine weeks. We assume that the Pregnancy Discrimination Act led to a significant increase in the number of women covered by such benefits as well as the benefit duration. Until our own survey was carried out, however, there were no data supporting this.

**Coverage at the End of the 1970s**

In short, a review of the status of maternity benefits in the late 1970s indicates that most employed women desiring to be mothers received quite limited if any accommodation from their employers. The practice of granting at least some unpaid maternity leave became fairly general practice, but even within the large corporate sector, the leave was limited to a half year or less, and, as we have indicated, probably far less outside of that sector. We estimate that the more important benefit, a leave with pay, was available to less than one-third of employed women in 1978, and this advantaged minority could count on only about six weeks of benefits. Maternity policies were undoubtedly "liberalized" over the course of the 1970s, but employer accommodation to childbearing was still very far from being a worker's right at the end of the decade.

In making our slightly lower estimate, we recognize that at the end of the 1970s, the general assumption seemed to be, however tenuously based and however incorrect, that about 40 percent of working women were entitled to some pay while on maternity leave. At the 1977 Senate hearings, *Discrimination on the Basis of Pregnancy*, Senator Birch Bayh testified that "63 percent of the civilian work force has some form of temporary disability coverage . . . and 60 percent of these plans covered pregnancy and childbirth."[11] Others, including the attorney for the U.S. Chamber of Commerce and a member of the American Academy of actuaries testified using the 40 percent figure, too. This figure had apparently come to be the prevailing wisdom used, although examination of the testimony provided does not offer strong documentation.

As we noted, though, the 1977 QES report indicated far lower coverage: 29 percent of those women working twenty or more hours per week. The 1978 Conference Board's estimate of 40 percent coverage may have encouraged a certain optimism even if a detailed look undercuts much sense of progress. The point to recognize, in addition to the focus on large companies with atypically "generous" policies, is that half the firms said that benefit coverage was provided through sickness benefits. Since the duration of these benefits is related to length of service, many young women workers had at best very limited benefits of two to four weeks at most.

We will return to the question of coverage for women workers, generally, later in this chapter, but for now we turn to a report of the current scene. What, then, is the picture in the early 1980s, two years after the Pregnancy Discrimination Act went into effect for all firms? What do most employers provide, not just the large corporations?

## PAID MATERNITY LEAVES IN THE PRIVATE SECTOR: THE 1980 PICTURE
### (The Columbia University Study)

In the American corporate welfare system, women employees, especially those with short service, can count on a paid leave of more than a week or two only if their company employs more than fifteen workers and has disability insurance, or if they work in one of the five states that provides or requires insurance against wage loss for non job-related disabilities during pregnancy and at the time of childbirth. (The policies of these states are considered in chapter 4.) Earlier studies have tended to include sick leave as an important source of income for women at the time of maternity, without acknowledging how inadequate such coverage is, even when and where available. We report here on the availability of sick leave, but its severe limitations as a maternity benefit must be recognized. We then consider the more substantial benefits associated with disability insurance, the only benefit that truly grants a paid leave.

### Paid Sick Leave

Paid sick leave offers important protections against illness during pregnancy but only very limited protection at the time of childbirth. Women with relatively brief service usually qualify for no more than two weeks and there is a maximum of four weeks for those with longer service (e.g., ten years or more). Only a very few companies provide a longer sick leave.

Two-thirds of the firms in our survey (150) have paid sick leaves. Banks and firms providing other financial services (80 percent) and very large firms with more than 500 employees (91 percent) are especially likely to provide sick leave (see table 3.7).

In half of the companies, eligibility for the minimum sick leave benefit comes with three months or less of service. Another quarter require four to six months of service to qualify,

**Table 3.7.** Availability of Paid Sick Leave, by Company
Characteristics

| Industry (selected categories) | | Sales ($ million)* | | Number of Employees | |
|---|---|---|---|---|---|
| Agriculture/mining/ | | | | | |
| construction | 61% (11) | 1 or less | 20% (1) | 1–25 | 69% (25) |
| Manufacturing | 56% (35) | 2–9 | 61% (47) | 26–99 | 60% (43) |
| Finance | 80% (45) | 10–49 | 56% (22) | 100–499 | 63% (39) |
| Trade and service | 59% (38) | 50+ | 71% (25) | 500+ | 91% (30) |

SOURCE: Columbia University Study.
NOTE: Percentages represent proportion with sick leave.
*Financial institutions are not included here.

and still another quarter require a year. It is important to note,
however, that even for women who do qualify, entitlement to
sick leave generally represents only a very small contribution
toward a paid maternity leave. For the women who meet the
minimum service requirement in the companies survey, the distribution is shown in table 3.8.

For the most part, more extensive benefits require a longer
period of minimum service to qualify. Although women with
substantial service (five or more years) are likely to qualify for
a longer sick leave, few companies provide more than a three-
or four-week maximum.

**Table 3.8.** Length of Sick Leave

| | |
|---|---|
| 2 days pay or less | 25% |
| 3–5 days | 25 |
| 6–10 days | 25 |
| 12+ days | 25 |
| | 100% |
| | (N = 121) |

## Disability Insurance

Clearly, for any paid leave that extends beyond a very few
weeks, the availability of disability insurance is an essential benefit. Let us point out here that short-term disability insurance
is the prevailing means for protecting the wages of employees
experiencing relatively brief nonoccupational disabilities (the

equivalent for exempt or salaried employees is an insured salary continuation plan). It constitutes the payment of a cash benefit representing a significant portion of wages lost at such times.

Of course the treatment of childbirth as a disability underscores the limited nature of employer accommodations to employees desiring children. Since the length of paid maternity leave is determined by a physician's certification of disability, female employees are certainly not encouraged to feel that they have any right to a specific amount of protected and paid time with their newborn. Rather, the focus is on the woman's physical condition and the time needed for her to convalesce after childbirth before resuming normal activities. As we shall discuss in the final chapter, this conception of maternity as a disability has significantly influenced the nature of maternity benefits and employer attitudes toward them.

Nonetheless, given prevailing medical practice, women with coverage under disability insurance can generally count on about six weeks of paid maternity leave if they have a normal pregnancy. Their entitlement is longer, of course, if the pregnancy or childbirth entails complications.

A significant proportion of firms have insurance plans that require a one-week waiting period before collecting benefits, if the employee is not hospitalized. When hospitalization is involved, close to half require no waiting period. About half the firms limit the maximum duration of payments to twenty-six weeks, while a small but significant group (more than one-quarter) set no limit, especially if the pregnancy involves complications. Where there is a waiting period before benefits commence, the availability of a paid sick leave becomes especially important.

What proportion of firms offer this benefit? *Approximately half of the firms in the sample offer disability insurance.*

As expected, the extent of coverage varies by the size of the firm as measured by the number of employees (see table 3.9). About one-third of the women at the very smallest firms in the sample (four to twenty-five employees) had coverage, probably an overstatement given the nature of our sample. By comparison, in each other category of firm size, about half or somewhat

**Table 3.9.** Availability of Disability Insurance, by Company
Characteristics

| Industry | | | Sales ($ million) | | Number of Employees | | |
|---|---|---|---|---|---|---|---|
| Agriculture/mining/ construction | 22% | (4) | $1–9 | 40% (32) | 4–25 | 33% | (12) |
| Manufacturing | 57% | (35) | | | 26–99 | 49% | (35) |
| Finance | 51% | (28) | $10+ | 60% (45) | 100–499 | 57% | (36) |
| Wholesale/retail service | 50% | (31) | | | 500–999 1,000+ | 56% | (18) |

SOURCE: Columbia University Study.
NOTE: Percentages represent proportion with disability insurance.

more of the companies extended disability insurance benefits.
Findings from QES, however, indicate that the likelihood of
maternity leave with pay (method of pay indeterminate: QES
does not have data on disability insurance per se) increases with
firm size.[12] Thus, rather than just a difference between small
firms and all others, larger firms were more likely to offer maternity coverage than were medium-sized firms. Our results
suggest either a problem with our data or a change in the patterns of benefit provision following the 1978 legislation. The
legislation may have led to an increase in provision among medium-sized firms that previously lagged behind the very large
firms in their response to maternity, while these latter firms did
not extend benefits beyond what was provided in the late 1970s.
That this, indeed, may be the case is a point we return to in
chapter 5.

Firm size as measured in sales volume also seems related to
whether firms will have disability insurance. As would be expected, firms with lower sales volume (i.e., under $10 million)
are less likely to have such coverage than firms with higher volume (over $10 million): 40 percent versus 60 percent.

When we turn to an exploration of how provision varies by
industry, the findings seem to suggest a less significant role.
Companies within the combined industrial category of agricul-
tural-mining-construction seem to lag behind the other industries, but apparently there are not significant differences among

manufacturing, finance, and trade and service. Other data indicate, however, that the trade and service industries tend toward a laggard status, largely attributable to the generally smaller size of firms in these industries (when we controlled for firm size, there was not much of an industry effect). We suspect that our sample of service and trade companies is not representative of firms within these industries, especially the smaller consumer-oriented companies.[13]

A quarter of the firms surveyed have some unionization, a significantly higher proportion than national data indicate.[14] This too suggests that our sample was somewhat biased. It is of interest, therefore, to note that unionization does not seem to make a significant difference in the provision of disability insurance, although it does with regard to other benefits (e.g., job-protected leave and health insurance). Neither the availability of a paid leave nor the duration of the leave seem to differ between unionized and nonunionized firms, any more than provision of disability insurance does. Whether this indicates a problem with our data, the growing standardization in maternity-related benefits, a weakening of the role of organized labor, or the lack of interest of organized labor in special provisions for women—or some combination—remains to be seen.

We noted earlier that paid sick leaves, although inadequate by themselves to provide sufficient protection against income loss at the time of maternity, do play a significant role in any overall protection at this time. Their availability assures a woman of financial protection during pregnancy if she is ill for a day or two; they provide some minimal protection when no disability insurance is available; and they provide the essential "bridge" for women working in firms requiring a week or more wait before disability benefit payments commence. Paid sick leaves are a necessary, but by themselves not sufficient, component of an adequate maternity policy. Firms having disability insurance are likely to have paid sick leaves, too, as can be seen in table 3.10.

### Combining Paid and Unpaid Leave

Firms with and without disability benefits have a similar variation in their policies relating to maximum leave. Most em-

**Table 3.10.** Firms with Paid Sick Leave and/or Disability Insurance

| | |
|---|---|
| Both benefits | 28% |
| Sick leaves only | 35 |
| Disability insurance only | 17 |
| Neither benefit | 20 |
| | 100% |

Source: Columbia University Study.

ployers (53 percent) who provide disability insurance permit leaves of two to three months; an equal proportion among those without disability insurance provide leaves of this length. Another significant proportion (15 percent) of the firms with disability insurance coverage describe the benefit duration as varying; these are likely to be two to three months also (see table 3.11). About 20 percent permit six months. In effect, then, relatively few firms with disability insurance offer the option of a leave that goes much beyond the typical medically prescribed disability period.

**Table 3.11.** Maximum Leave, by Disability Insurance Coverage

| Maximum Months Leave | Disability Insurance | | | |
|---|---|---|---|---|
| | Have coverage | | Lack coverage | |
| 0 | 1* | 1 | 1 | 1 |
| 1 | 7 | 8 | 6 | 6 |
| 2 | 21 | 25 | 27 | 30 |
| 3 | 32 | 38 | 26 | 29 |
| 4 | 2 | 3 | 2 | 3 |
| 5 | 1 | 1 | 1 | 1 |
| 6 | 17 | 21 | 20 | 22 |
| 9 | 1 | 1 | 0 | 0 |
| 12 | 3 | 4 | 8 | 9 |
| Varies | 15 | — | 8 | — |
| | 100% | 100%† | 99% | 100%† |
| | (88) | (73) | (85) | (77) |

Source: Columbia University Study.
*Either coding error or interpreted as in addition to disability time.
†Percentages computed with exclusion of the "varies" category from base.

The option of receiving a partial wage replacement for two to three months and then taking several more months of unpaid but fully job-protected leave appears open to relatively few women. Indeed, our data raise questions about the finding of the earlier Conference Board survey, in which 77 percent of the responding firms granted six months or more of leave. (As we mentioned earlier, the very large firms may have curtailed their leave policies. We return to this in chapter 5.) At most, a quarter of the firms in our sample permit leaves of six months or more. Moreover, most of this group grants a six-month leave; only about one-tenth of the entire sample permit a longer leave.

## Employer Expectations

Although no clear trend is evident to employers asked about the inclinations of women to return to work after childbirth (see table 3.12), most employers do expect that most employees will return to their jobs at the end of their leaves. Of course, many employers may see no clear trend simply because they have had so little experience with women going on leave. This is, after all, a relatively recent phenomenon. Nor is there any factor that

**Table 3.12.** Employers' Expectations of Percentage of Women on Leave Returning to Work

| Percentage of Employees Expected to Return | Percentage of Employers with This Expectation |
| --- | --- |
| 75–100% | 43% |
| 50–75% | 26 |
| 25–49% | 13 |
| 0–24% | 19 |
| | 100% (160) |
| *Is this trend increasing?* | |
| Notable increase | 31% |
| No notable increase | 31 |
| Don't know | 39 |
| | 100% (156) |

SOURCE: Columbia University Study.
NOTE: Percentages rounded.

seems to correlate especially closely with the perceived likelihood of women returning to work, not even the availability of longer or more generous leaves.

In any case, our data suggest that the number of women on leave is not large enough to cause widespread difficulties. The great majority of the smallest firms—the firms that might be expected to encounter the greatest difficulty in making adjustment—had no or only one employee on leave. And we suspect that firms without any experience (or any recent experience) with maternity leaves were especially likely not to respond to our survey.

## AN OVERVIEW

All of the statistical detail provided in the preceding pages of this chapter should not mislead: a fully accurate picture of the availability of maternity-related benefits is not now available. We have brought together the best data gathered to date, including our original survey data, but all sources of information are in some significant way limited. Indeed, it seems a telling measure of the disjointed nature of American maternity "policy," and even of the lack of concern until recent years, that so little is reliably known. Nonetheless, even though we are unable to draw the benefit picture in precise detail, the main features of this picture can be broadly sketched.

We have identified three fundamental components of a minimally responsive maternity policy: health insurance, a job-protected leave, and some wage replacement during leaves. In brief, here is where we stand on each of these components:

*Health insurance:* A third of all full-time female workers in the private sector, including almost one-third of those who are not married (divorced and separated as well as single) do not have health insurance; and part-time workers as well as very young women are especially likely to lack coverage. We cannot specify the size of the gap in coverage because the extent to which uncovered married women are included within their husband's plan is unknown. Given existing data, it seems that at least 10 percent of all working women in their childbearing years lack coverage from some source.

*Job-protected leave:* A major development of the 1970s is that a short leave at childbirth—with seniority and pension rights protection as well as some assurance of retaining the same or comparable job—has become available to many women workers. Some three-quarters of women working at least twenty hours a week are eligible for such a leave, though eligibility is much lower at small firms. Overall, it appears that considerably more than half of all firms limit leaves to three months or less, with two or three months being the most common policy. Even in the large corporate sector of the economy, the great majority of leaves are restricted to a half year or less. The details of these leave policies—the formality of a guarantee, length of service required for eligibility, and the procedures involved in determining a comparable job—all appear to vary widely. Again, the corporate sector is not the model for the rest of the work force; a woman's entitlements seem less generous and less formally established in small businesses. Few companies have formal policies relating to extended paternity leaves, though a notable minority informally allow a few days off, usually as part of sick leave.

*Paid leaves:* The third component remains the least adequate. By recent law, pregnant employees must be treated the same as employees with any other temporary disability, and thus women working at firms with short-term sickness or disability insurance have at least some paid maternity leave. While paid sick leave is common—perhaps two-thirds or so of all firms offer it—women with brief service usually receive less than two weeks of pay and those with longer service are usually eligible for less than a month. Usually, only upon the availability of disability insurance is there a paid leave that extends beyond a few weeks. We may roughly estimate that somewhat less than half of all firms offer this benefit. Again, women working at very small firms are notably disadvantaged; at most a third have disability coverage. Under prevailing conventions relating to this disability, childbirth usually entails six weeks of insurance payments.

The option of receiving at least partial wage replacement for even two months or so and then taking several more months of unpaid but fully protected leave appears available to relatively few women. Perhaps a fifth of all firms offer this.

Progress has certainly been made, largely under the impetus of government regulation, but the progress has been highly uneven and far less than many believe. Any attempts to assess private sector provisions for maternity, and subsequently to improve them, must recognize the pattern of inequalities. Women employed in smaller businesses generally are entitled to less generous treatment than their counterparts in the large corporate sector. It is misleading to see large corporate practice as typical of the private sector. As we will detail in the following chapter, public sector practices lead to unequal entitlements as well.

# 4. THE BENEFIT PICTURE: STATE AND FEDERAL PROVISIONS

By necessity, any assessment of U.S. maternity policy must center on private sector practices, especially disability insurance coverage. That is the cornerstone, the unique emphasis of American policy. Although there is no national statutory maternity benefit in the United States, there are some public sector requirements in the form of state statutes, and there are important entitlements for federal employees as well. These provisions are reviewed in this chapter. Only a minority of women are affected by these provisions, but they indicate the different arrangements that are already accommodated within the American system and point to some of the different sorts of arrangements that may be contemplated.

We should note that the employee-level data reported in chapter 3, especially the Quality of Employment Survey (QES), report benefits based on both private and public employment. The company-level reports integrate state requirements in those instances in which statutes mandate benefits that cover maternity, in some instances reporting benefits from state programs and, in others, company programs that permit the company to bypass the state requirements.

## STATUTORY BENEFITS PROVIDED BY STATES

Five states (California, Hawaii, New Jersey, New York, and Rhode Island) and Puerto Rico have temporary disability insurance laws to provide income when people are unable to work because of disabilities not due to job-related accidents or illness (see table 4.1).

## Rhode Island

Rhode Island was the state that enacted the first compulsory temporary disability insurance (TDI) program in 1942. The first benefit payments were made on April 1, 1943. Pregnancy and maternity were covered fairly early in the program, and in 1964 the maximum number of weekly payments was extended from twelve to fourteen weeks. Also in 1964, the TDI taxable wage base was increased from $3,600 to $4,800, where it remained until January 1, 1982. In 1969, as a consequence of an operating deficit in the program, pregnancy benefits for normal pregnancy and deliveries were changed from fourteen weekly payments to a lump sum maternity payment, limited to $250 but increased to $500 in 1980. During the 1970s, total maternity benefits remained fairly steady in the state; however, a sizable increase in the number of such payments did occur in 1979 and in 1980. As a result of the increases in both the number and amounts of payments, the latest expenditure data indicate that the costs in those years were somewhere between $2.3 and $2.6 million.

In 1980, the Rhode Island legislature created a commission to study TDI and report findings and recommendations to the General Assembly by March 1, 1981. Of particular interest is that the focus of this commission's work was on the sickness and maternity benefit entitlement. Included in the recommendations of the commission were the following:

1. eliminate the lump sum maternity payments and consider pregnancy as an illness, with benefit entitlements determined on an individual basis;
2. raise the TDI maximum weekly benefit amount to an amount equal to 60 percent of the average weekly wage of TDI-covered employment;
3. increase the TDI dependency allowance from $3 to $5 per child up to a maximum of four dependents;

**Table 4.1.** State Non-Occupational Disability Laws (1983)

| | Employers Covered | Permissible Plans | Employee/Employer Contributions | Benefit Duration and Benefit Levels† | Maternity |
|---|---|---|---|---|---|
| CALIFORNIA★ Unemployment Compensation Disability Benefits (UCD). Employment Development Dept. Sacramento, Calif. 95814. | Employers of one or more employees. | 1. State Plan or 2. Private Voluntary Plan may be insured or self-insured, but needs majority consent of employees to be set up. These plans must meet all State Plan requirements, and exceed at least one of the requirements. | Employee contributions consist of .8% of first $17,000 annual earnings. No employer contributions are mandated; however, employers are permitted to make contributions on behalf of the employee. | Benefits are based on schedule using quarterly earnings figures. Maximum $175, minimum $50, 39-week benefit duration. | Covered the same as any other disability. |
| HAWAII★ Temporary Disability Insurance Law (TDI). Dept. of Labor and Industrial Relations. P.O. Box 3769, Honolulu, Hawaii 96812. | Employers of one or more employees. | 1. No State Plan. 2. Private Plan may be insured or self-insured and must equal or exceed statutory requirements. No employee consent necessary. | Employees must contribute the lesser of ½ of 1% of statewide average weekly wage or ½ the cost subject to a maximum of $1.61 weekly. Employers must pay the balance of costs incurred. | Benefits consist of 55% of average weekly wage rounded to next higher dollar, maximum $1.77. For average weekly wage less than $26, benefit equal to average weekly wage, with $14 maximum. | Covered the same as any other disability. |

**Table 4.1.** State Non-Occupational Disability Laws (1983) (*Continued*)

| | Employers Covered | Permissible Plans | Employee/Employer Contributions | Benefit Duration and Benefit Levels† | Maternity |
|---|---|---|---|---|---|
| **NEW JERSEY***<br>Temporary Disability Benefits (TDI).<br>Dept. of Labor and Industry.<br>P.O. Box 825<br>Trenton, N.J. 08625. | Employers with minimum annual payroll of $1,000 with one or more employees. | 1. State Plan or<br>2. Private Plan may be insured or self-insured and must equal or exceed State Plan requirements. If plan is contributory, majority consent of employees is necessary. | For both employers and employees, the contribution level is ½ of 1% of first $8800 annual earnings.<br><br>Employers who have contributed to the Fund during the three prior years are subject to "experience rating." Their contributions may vary from .1% to 1.1%. | Benefits consist of 66⅔% of average weekly earnings to next higher $1, maximum $158, minimum $10. | Covered the same as any other disability. |
| **NEW YORK***<br>Disability Benefits Law (DBL).<br>Workers' Compensation Board.<br>2 World Trade Center,<br>New York, N.Y. 10047. | Employers of one or more employees (4 or more domestics) on each of 30 working days in calendar year. | 1. State Plan or<br>2. Private Plan may be insured or self-insured and must equal or exceed State Plan requirements. No employee consent necessary. | Employee contributions are ½ of 1% of first $60 weekly earnings. Employers must pay the balance of costs for "standard" plans. | Benefits are 50% of average weekly earnings, maximum $95, minimum $20 or employee's average weekly wage, if less. | Covered the same as any other disability. |

| | Coverage | Type of Plan | Financing | Benefits | Maternity |
|---|---|---|---|---|---|
| **PUERTO RICO** Disability Benefits ACT (DBA). Bureau of Employment Security. Hato Rey, Puerto Rico 00917. | Employers of one or more employees. | 1. State Plan or 2. Private Plan may be insured or self-insured and must equal or exceed State Plan requirements. Majority employee consent needed to set up plan if contributory. | Both employers and employees pay .3% of the first $9,000 in wages. | Benefits set at 60% of weekly earnings: maximum $104, minimum $7 (on base annual income of $150). Death benefit: $3,000 AD & D benefit up to $3,000. | Covered the same as any other disability. |
| **RHODE ISLAND** Temporary Disability Insurance Benefits (TDI). Dept. of Employment Security. 24 Mason Street Providence, R.I. 02903. | Employers of one or more employees. | 1. State Plan only; no private plan plans allowed. 2. No Private Plans allowed, except where Private Plan is a supplement to the State Plan. | Employees contribute 1.2% of first $9,200 annual earnings. No employer contributions are mandated. | Benefit based on 55% of individual average weekly earnings: maximum $151, minimum $37; plus $5 per dependent child (up to age 18) up to $20. (This maximum is recomputed annually and is equal to 60% of the average weekly wage of all workers covered by TDI.) | Covered the same as any other disability. |

Source: Johnson and Higgins, *Comparative Analysis of Non-occupational Disability Laws*, January 1983. Reprinted with permission. (Minor modifications based on personal communications with state officials.)

*Recipients of unemployment benefits can interrupt or obtain additional protection if they become disabled while unemployed.

†Benefits begin on 8th day for disabilities due to accidents and on 8th day for disabilities due to sickness with a 26-week maximum duration for all states except California. Benefits are tax-free.

4. relate minimum earnings requirement for TDI benefit eligibility to the Rhode Island statutory minimum wage; and
5. adopt a flexible, taxable wage base relating to the average annual wage of TDI covered employment and concurrently reduce the employee tax rate from 1.5 to 1.2 percent.

These recommendations were all approved and incorporated into legislation that went into effect July 1, 1981. As a consequence, pregnancy is now treated under the state's TDI program the same as any nonwork-related illness. The estimated benefit duration for a normal pregnancy and delivery is ten weeks. The woman's physician must certify the disability due to the pregnancy both before and after delivery. Claimants must have earned at least $62 in each of twenty weeks in the prior year or received total wages of at least $3,720 in order to qualify for TDI. (The base period is the first 52 weeks of the fifty-three-week period before the initial claim is filed.) Three weeks of full benefits are allowed for every five weeks worked in a base period up to a maximum of twenty-six full weeks in a benefit year. The tax rate beginning January 1, 1982 went from 1.5 percent down to 1.2 percent, and the taxable wage base was increased and set at an amount equal to 70 percent of the average annual wages for all workers covered by the TDI act. The cost of the benefit is estimated to increase by about 5.2 percent. However, this includes all the recommended changes, not just that change defining normal pregnancy as qualifying for this benefit.

In 1980, the average weekly benefit amount, excluding lump sum maternity benefits, was $77.73. Approximately 4,300 women who received a lump sum benefit in 1980 were eligible to receive weekly benefits for pregnancy. In 1981, the taxable wage base was raised to $7,800. For taxpayers who earn less than $6,000, their contribution to TDI would be less than the sum they had been paying before. For those earning more, their costs would go up. Regardless, however, this revised plan should lead to a significantly improved benefit system for employees and one that is much more closely integrated with the unemployment insurance program than previously.

No private plans are allowed in Rhode Island, except as a supplement to the state plan.

## California

As in all the states with temporary disability insurance, the California Disability Insurance (DI) Law, the second oldest such law in the country, dating from 1946, is designed to protect workers against the loss of wages when unable to perform their usual work because of illness or injury not related to their jobs.

In 1974, the DI law specifically limited pregnancy and maternity benefits to disabilities related to complications. In 1977, coverage for normal pregnancy was added for up to three weeks before and three weeks after birth. In 1979, the law was amended to permit a maximum benefit of six weeks, regardless of whether it was taken immediately preceding or following childbirth. In 1979, the definition of disability was changed to follow the federal law, and thus to include any injury or illness resulting from pregnancy, childbirth, or a related condition. New legislation eliminated the six-weeks cap, although six weeks still remained the standard post-childbirth benefit duration for a normal pregnancy. From January 1, 1981, pregnancy and childbirth have been viewed as the same as any other temporary disability and benefits permitted accordingly, depending on what the certifying physician states.

The California DI program has two insurance plans, a state plan and a voluntary plan. State plan coverage is mandated for insured employees unless they have chosen voluntary plans or claimed religious exemptions. A voluntary plan is a private plan approved by the director of the Employment Development Department, the agency responsible for administering the state plan. A voluntary plan may be substituted for the state plan if it matches state benefits, provides at least one greater benefit, and costs the employee no more than the state plan. About 6 percent of the state disability insurance is provided through voluntary plans.

Employers and employee groups may establish voluntary plans with the mutual consent of the employer and a majority of the employees. Employees may choose state plan coverage even though a voluntary plan is available where they work. Most of the 379 voluntary plans, covering a little more than 469,000 workers in a covered labor force of about 8.8 million are in banks, insurance companies, and retail stores.

Basic benefits in 1981 ranged from a minimum of $30 per week to a maximum of $154. As of January 1, 1982, the maximum benefit increased to $175 per week; the minimum to $50. There is a seven-day nonpayable waiting period before receipt of the benefit unless the person is admitted to a hospital or treated in a surgical clinic or unit, provided that the disability lasts at least eight days. If the disability lasts twenty-one days or longer, the waiting period is waived and the benefit is paid retroactively.

DI benefits may be paid for a maximum of 39 weeks. Since pregnancy is now treated the same as any other temporary disability, benefit duration varies by the woman's condition and type of work. Where a normal pregnancy is involved, most of the variations in duration occur in relation to the period before anticipated childbirth. Thus, for example, office workers can work up to the ninth month (or even until they go into labor if they wish); however, construction workers or agricultural workers may stop work in their seventh month if so ordered to by their physician. In contrast, postpartum leaves are far more standardized: Six to eight weeks is the prevailing pattern, with six weeks the most usual. In 1978 the average benefit period for a normal delivery was 4.7 weeks, for a caesarean 8.9 weeks, and for all pregnancy and childbirth related disabilities, 5 weeks.

These DI benefits are payable when an insured employee cannot work because of sickness or injury not related to his or her job; or when the employee is entitled to workers' compensation at a rate less than the daily DI benefit amount.

To qualify for DI benefits, an employee must have been working for a covered employer (any employer with a payroll in excess of $100 in a calendar quarter), have been paid wages totaling at least $300 during the twelve months preceding the disability, and have filed a certificate of disability signed by an authorized medical or religious practitioner. Excluded from coverage in the California DI program are some domestic workers, most governmental employees, employees of interstate railroads and employees of some nonprofit organizations. Entitled to elect DI coverage are self-employed persons, individuals in family employment, bargaining units of government employers, and individuals who are themselves employers.

Domestic workers are now eligible for coverage if they earned $1,000 or more in the previous quarter from one employer. New legislation is expected to lower this minimum to $750. Ultimately, the hope is to treat domestic workers the same as all others.

State employees are covered under a Non-Industrial Disability Insurance program (NDI) that is a wage continuation program completely paid by the state. Weekly benefits are equal to one-half gross pay up to a maximum of $125 per week for a period not to exceed twenty-six weeks after exhaustion of sick leave. Over $6 million in NDI payments were made in 1980.

In 1981 the California civilian labor force was estimated to include 10.7 million workers, with 8.8 million covered by DI. The projections for 1982 are a labor force of 11 million with 9 million covered under DI, a coverage rate of about 82 percent.

Administered by the State Employment Development Department, these state plans are financed entirely by California workers through a payroll tax on their earnings. However, two hundred employers, covering 200,000 employees, pay the contribution as a fringe benefit. The tax rate for 1982 was .8 percent of the first $17,000 in annual wages. Except for one year, the tax rate had been a constant 1 percent from 1946 to 1980. It was reduced because of a substantial surplus in the DI fund. On January 1, 1982, when the wage base was raised, the tax rate was increased slightly for those with wages between $14,900 and $17,000 and a new formula established so that, when the wage base increases in the future, the benefit level will also. The tax rate will be adjusted, too, to avoid building up too large a surplus.

Since the DI program has covered normal pregnancy and maternity, there has been a fairly steady increase in nonhospital claims and benefits (see table 4.2)

**Table 4.2.** Disability Benefits and Claims in California After Inclusion of Pregnancy and Childbirth (1978)

| Types of Benefits and Claims | State Plan (thousand) | Voluntary Plan (thousand) | Percent Change, 1977–78 | |
|---|---|---|---|---|
| | | | State | Voluntary |
| Basic benefits | 406.2 | 40.8 | +7 | +10 |
| Claims with basic benefit only | 233.7 | 20.7 | +4 | +10 |
| Claims with basic and hospital benefits | 311.8 | 25.1 | −2 | ±2 |
| Claims with hospital benefits only | 20.6 | 4.2 | −20 | −10 |
| Average weekly basic benefit | $100.00 | $141.49 | +10 | +11 |

Out of a total of more than 600,000 temporary disability claims filed in 1978, 50,175, or about 8 percent, were filed for pregnancy, childbirth, and related conditions.* Of these, 46,185 (92 percent of the total) were for normal deliveries, a 41 percent increase from 1977 (32,100). Of the overall total, more than 43,000 were filed by women aged 22 to 34. In 1980 the total number of temporary disability claims processed remained about the same or even a little lower (about 600,000). However, pregnancy claims increased to somewhere between 10 and 15 percent of the total. The average weekly state plan benefit paid in December 1980 was $115.96. (Data for the average voluntary plan benefit were not available.)

### New Jersey

New Jersey's TDI legislation was passed in 1948. Disabilities related to pregnancy were excluded initially from protection under this legislation. However, the law was amended, subse-

---

*In 1967, only 392 claims were filed, all for complications of pregnancy, a dramatically different figure for a time when fewer women were at work, and, more important, when normal pregnancies were not covered by DI. Even complicated conditions were infrequently entitled to benefits at that time.

quently, to provide that pregnancy be defined as a sickness during the four weeks immediately preceding the expected birth and the four weeks immediately following termination of pregnancy (the period during which unemployment benefits could not be paid). Beginning in 1975, claims based on medical complications of pregnancy have been payable in the same way as all other claims, up to a maximum of twenty-six weeks. This applies to the state plan, private plans, as well as disability while receiving unemployment benefits. Following passage of the 1978 federal legislation the specific "4-4" limitation was eliminated in 1979. Yet there still is a prevailing standard for the benefit duration, as indicated below.

TDI, under the Temporary Disability Law in New Jersey, provides income support to a person temporarily unable to work because of a nonoccupational injury or illness. All workers covered by unemployment insurance are also covered by a mandatory disability insurance system. In 1980 coverage was extended to state employees; and other governmental entities may elect coverage for their employees. Workers may be covered by the state disability insurance plan or by a private plan approved by the New Jersey Division of Unemployment and Disability Insurance, which must have the same provisions as state plan coverage or better.

The New Jersey state plan covers women disabled while on the job or within fourteen days of leaving the job, regardless of the reasons for leaving. Supplementing this is the unemployment plan, established to provide protection for the ten weeks around the time of maternity when unemployment benefits would be lost, because women receiving these benefits are defined as "not available for work" at that time. This plan covers workers disabled more than fourteen days after leaving work. Initially all workers were covered, regardless of the reason for leaving their jobs, but since 1980, workers leaving work voluntarily have not been covered. Women leaving their jobs for maternity reasons, intending to return some months after giving birth and then not finding a job, could qualify. Workers who become pregnant while receiving unemployment benefits could receive a combination of unemployment benefits, plus "disability during unemployment" benefit, for a maximum of thirty-nine weeks (rather than the twenty-six-week maximum permitted under unemployment benefits alone).

There is no job security provision in the New Jersey TDI law. Employers are required to provide job security to a pregnant woman only to the same extent as for other temporarily disabled workers. A worker who leaves her job for maternity purposes intending to return within a specified agreed-on time after childbirth, could, therefore, qualify for unemployment benefits if her prior job were unavailable.

Under the state plan, the basic weekly cash benefit is equal to two-thirds of average weekly wage during the eight weeks prior to the onset of the disability, subject to a maximum of one-half the statewide average weekly wage. The maximum payable on disabilities beginning in 1981 was $133 or a maximum of $3,458 for twenty-six weeks; in 1982 it was $145.

The maximum duration of the benefit is twenty-six weeks. Although the full period is available when there are pregnancy or childbirth complications, the prevailing standard for normal pregnancies and deliveries is four weeks immediately before anticipated birth and six weeks after. For caesarean births the standard is eight to ten weeks after birth. Physicians who certify that a woman is disabled for longer than the "standard" are likely to be called personally by agency personnel and asked why. There is a seven-day waiting period before qualifying for disability benefits; however, if the disability lasts for three or more consecutive weeks, benefits are paid retroactively for the first week. The average duration of pregnancy claims under both types of state plans (for working women and those receiving unemployment benefits) in 1976 was about 8 weeks; currently, the average is estimated as between nine and ten weeks.

To be eligible for disability insurance benefits under the state plan, one must be working for an employer who is covered by disability insurance. During the year preceding the date of the claim, the woman must have worked at least seventeen weeks with earnings of $15 or more in each of these weeks, or have earned $2,200 or more during the preceding year. She must be

**Table 4.3.** Pregnancy Disability
Claims in New Jersey (State Plan)

| Year | Number of Claims |
|------|------------------|
| 1974 | 8,056 |
| 1975 | 7,683 |
| 1976 | 5,944 |
| 1980 | 3,508 |

SOURCE: Statement of James A. Ware, Assistant Commissioner, New Jersey Department of Labor and Industry, Testimony, *Discrimination on the Basis of Pregnancy*, 1977, p. 172.
NOTE: Although data are not available for claims under private plans, there is no reason to assume any difference in trends of proportionate claims, given that close to two-thirds of the labor force is covered under the state plan and less than one-quarter under private plans.

under the care of one of several types of health professionals who certify to the disability.

Almost all privately employed workers in New Jersey are covered, as well as all state employees, including teachers. Domestic workers are eligible, too, on the same basis as others. City employees may elect coverage, but most do not. Government workers, however, must exhaust all accumulated sick leave benefits before disability benefits can be paid. More specifically, out of a labor force of about 3 million workers in June 1981, the state plan covered 1.9 million and private plans .7 million, leaving only 400,000 workers, or 16 percent of the labor force, uncovered.

In 1980, 14,457 disability claims were filed under the state disability plan and 6,176 under the unemployment plan. About 17 percent of the claims load is for pregnancy.[1]

The temporary disability benefit is funded through a payroll tax that both employers and employees pay. This tax is .5 percent of wages for each up to a maximum of $8,200 in 1982. This means that the maximum tax payable for employees for the year is $41.

Despite the increase in the numbers and type of employees covered by disability insurance in New Jersey, there has been a steady decline in the number of pregnancy claims (see table 4.3), apparently reflecting birth rate declines.

## New York

Until the New York State Court of Appeals ruled otherwise in a 1976 decision, disability benefits were payable only for disabilities that occurred after a woman had worked in covered employment for at least two consecutive weeks following the termination of pregnancy. According to that decision, all employers subject to the New York State Human Rights Law—those with four or more employees—were required to provide wage maintenance for pregnancy disability to the same extent as provided for all other types of disabilities under the Disability Benefits Law.[2] Legislation amending the State Disability Law (passed initially in 1949) to take account of this decision was passed in 1977. A 1981 amendment subsequently repealed the section of the 1977 law that limited the benefit covering normal pregnancy to a period of eight weeks. In effect, this new amendment eliminated the distinction between pregnancy-related disabilities and other disabilities with respect to eligibility and entitlement under the law.

According to New York State law, disability benefits are temporary cash benefits payable to eligible wage earners when they are disabled by an off-the-job injury or illness. The original legislation was passed in 1950. Supplementing the Workers' Compensation Law and administered by the Workers' Compensation Board, the Disability Benefits Law insures protection for wage earners by providing for weekly cash benefits to replace, in part, wages lost because of injuries or illnesses that do not arise out of and in the course of employment. Disability benefits are also provided to an unemployed claimant to replace those Unemployment Insurance Benefits lost because of an illness or injury.

With few exceptions, the Disability Law requires that all private employers offer what is referred to as "statutory coverage" or "plan coverage." Statutory coverage refers to the minimum benefits required by law, and plan coverage refers to a package devised by the employer and certified as equivalent to the statutory coverage by the chairman of the Workers' Compensation Board. Plans may be either self-insured or insured with an authorized insurance company.

Plan benefits may vary, so long as they meet minimum standards. Where plan benefits are not provided, a worker was entitled to receive the following statutory benefits in 1981: cash benefits constituting 50 percent of average weekly wages (based on the last eight weeks of employment) with a maximum benefit of $95 per week. (Recent legislation will gradually raise this to $145 a week by 1986.)

The maximum duration of the benefit is 26 weeks. Since the recent elimination of the eight-week specification concerning maternity, no set standard exists and the experience is too recent to provide any data. In 1980, the average benefit duration for a normal pregnancy was 6.9 weeks. Program staff anticipate an increase to twelve to fifteen weeks per claim, given the amended legislation, but have no data to support their projections.

Workers qualify for disability benefits if they are working or have worked recently for a covered employer for at least four consecutive weeks, have become disabled, and are under the care of one of several types of health or certified religious professionals who validates the disability.* Certain categories of employees are excluded from mandatory coverage, including government workers (federal, state, and local), farm workers, ministers (priests and rabbis), several categories of employees of nonprofit organizations, and so forth.

An employer of one or more persons on each of thirty days in any calendar year becomes a covered employer four weeks after the thirtieth day of such employment. However, employers of personal or domestic employees in a private home become a covered employer only if they employ four or more such workers. (Proposed legislation would require coverage for all domestics working forty or more hours per week.)

Unemployed workers receiving unemployment insurance benefits who become disabled after more than four weeks but

---

*For example, Christian Science healers.

within twenty-six weeks of employment are entitled to disability benefits as soon as they are disqualified from unemployment benefits (as in New Jersey).

About 6 million employees were included in 1978 under either the statutory or plan coverage. Assuming that this figure remained constant, about 82 percent of the 1980 labor force of 7.3 million in New York had such coverage.

Disability benefits are paid for either jointly by employer and employee or solely by the employer. Where the employer is providing statutory benefits the employee may be required to contribute .5 percent of the first $60 of weekly wages up to a maximum of $.30 per week. Where plan benefits are provided, the employer may pay the entire cost, or, if employees contribute, employers must add their own contributions to cover the whole cost if it is higher.

In 1978, the first full year for which data are available for pregnancy claims (and the latest year for which data are available), total benefits paid for partial wage replacement amounted to about $16 million or 4 percent of the total cash benefit payments for all disabilities. Of this amount, $12.5 million was for normal pregnancy claims (eight weeks or less) and the remainder for pregnancy complication claims. The total number of pregnancy claims was 24,400 (21,300 for normal pregnancy) out of a total of 826,000 claims overall, or 3 percent of the total.

In 1978–79, 10,000 complaints were filed with the New York State Human Rights Commission regarding pregnancy discrimination related to receipt of benefit. In 1980, 216 complaints were filed. These figures point to the extent to which the provision of disability benefits at the time of pregnancy has become established policy. The obvious inference is that compliance has become general.

One question now is what the impact will be of the elimination of the eight-week standard. Workers' Compensation staff expect the claims for longer benefits to increase. At the same time, many employers seem to be pressuring for a shorter period of disability. Whether this will result in an upsurge of complaints remains to be seen. Indeed, most complaints now coming before the commission have to do with job termination or restriction of benefits, clearly increasingly important issues in the maternity policy field.

## Hawaii

Hawaii was the first state to provide benefits explicitly for a normal pregnancy, although the TDI programs in Rhode Island covered pregnancy even earlier. Initially (1969), the Hawaii statute denied benefits during pregnancy except when complications resulted in total disability. However, the law was amended in May 1973 to grant benefits to any individual in current employment who suffers disability resulting from pregnancy or termination of pregnancy. Pregnancy and childbirth were to be covered in the same way that disabilities from other causes are covered. Disability is defined as "total inability of an employee to perform the duties of his employment caused by sickness, pregnancy, or accident other than a work injury. . . ."

The legislation mandates an employer plan for all employers with one or more employees, which can take the form of self-insurance, an insured plan, or other kinds of coverage via union contract. There is no state plan, as such.

The law provides the same maximum duration for receipt of disability benefits for pregnancy and childbirth as for all disabilities, namely 26 weeks. The basic benefit provided is 55 percent of the average weekly wage, after a seven-day waiting period, with a minimum benefit of $14 and a maximum of $168. Because of the nature of the plan there are no data concerning an average benefit. The maximum benefit duration is twenty-six weeks, but the specific time length depends on the nature of the disability and a physician's certificate.

Eligibility is limited to employees currently working in covered employment, or who have worked within two weeks prior to becoming disabled, and who would have worked if not for the disability. To be eligible for Temporary Disability Insurance (TDI) benefits, an employee must also have worked for at least fourteen weeks in the year preceding the onset of disability and have received pay for twenty or more hours in each of these weeks. Finally, the employee must be in the care of a licensed physician or other specified health care professional, who in turn must certify the nature and extent of the employee's disability.

Virtually all employees in the state are covered except for federal workers and a few occupations (e.g., insurance agents, family workers). Domestic servants are excluded only if they earn less than $225 a quarter. Financing is shared equally by employer and employee, with employee contributions of no more than .5 percent of weekly wages; the maximum wage base is $305.36 weekly. If the costs are higher, employers must pay the additional amount.

In an initial study of the Hawaiian experience, which reported on the first two years following the legislation's implementation, coverage of pregnancy and maternity increased neither the benefit costs for women employees nor the average disability benefit duration for women over what had prevailed earlier. The average benefit duration for women, which included disability due to accident and sickness as well as pregnancy, was 4.4 weeks, lower than the 5.1 week average for male employees.[3]

### Summary of Provision for States with TDI

Five states (California, Hawaii, New Jersey, New York, and Rhode Island) provide TDI for employees at the time of normal pregnancy and delivery. New Jersey covers state government employees but not local government workers. In California, state employees are covered under a special fringe benefit, but one that is less generous than the state plan for private sector employees. No government workers are covered in New York or Rhode Island. All these states also cover eligible workers receiving unemployment insurance. Thus, about 82 percent of the labor force in these states are covered under some form of TDI.

The peak period for establishing these programs was in the 1940s. All but the Puerto Rican legislation (1969) and Hawaiian (1969) date from these years. During the 1950s a number of states conducted studies, held hearings, and considered bills, but there were no laws enacted until 1960–70, and no activity since then. Why the flurry occurred when it did and why other states have not followed is of interest, but no explanation exists.[4]

Those public employees who are not protected by disability protection in these and other states are likely, however, to be subject to maternity policies similar to those of the federal government.

## FEDERAL EMPLOYEES AND MATERNITY

The federal government's policy on maternity is that "an agency shall grant sick leave . . . when the employee . . . is incapacitated for the performance of duties by . . . pregnancy and confinement. . . ."[5] The current policy was first established in 1974 by the U.S. Civil Services Commission in an effort at eliminating any provisions that might suggest or generate different treatment for pregnant employees than for others who experience temporary disabilities requiring them to be away from work. Thus, federal agencies are directed to apply the same leave policies, regulations, and procedures in granting leave for maternity reasons as are applicable to requests for leave generally.

Leave for maternity reasons is chargeable to sick leave or a combination of sick leave, annual leave, and leave without pay. Sick leave, earned at the rate of thirteen days a year, may be used to cover the time required for physical examinations, illness during pregnancy, and the time immediately following childbirth. Advance sick leave may also be granted, if necessary, for employees expecting to return to work. After delivery and recuperation, additional leave requirements for adjustment or to make arrangements for child care may be met by the use of available annual leave (earned at the rate of thirteen, twenty, or twenty-six days per year depending on length of service). Annual leave may also be advanced if requested and approved. However, neither accrued nor advance annual leave in excess of the period of actual incapacitation are guaranteed, and indeed, may be denied when it would result in a serious handicap to the work of the office.[6]

In addition, for the employee who intends to return to work after childbirth, leave without pay may be granted for "adjustment" and child care reasons. Determination of the length of the leave is made on an individual basis by the employee, her physician, and the leave-approving officers. It would seem that a paid five-week paid leave would be available at the very minimum, with six weeks a strong possibility, even for workers with brief service. This would, however, preclude any other sick leave or annual leave for the year in which maternity occurs, and possibly for some portion of the next year.

Sick leave and annual leave are fully paid, and ensure the continuity of all benefits. Benefits also are continued for employees on leave without pay status for up to one year.

Employees also have full health insurance coverage for pregnancy and maternity. In addition, the same or a comparable job is guaranteed the employee out for maternity reasons. Annual leave, advance annual leave, or leave without pay also may be granted male employees for paternity reasons at the time their wives give birth.

Because pregnancy and maternity leaves are defined as the same as any other type of leave, no data are available on the numbers of women taking such leaves or trends over time.

## SUMMING UP THE COVERAGE PICTURE

In assessing the implications of the statutory provision at the state level for national coverage, our conclusions can be only tentative. Our survey subsample of employers from California, Hawaii, New Jersey, New York, and Rhode Island is very small. It may be that while some minimum protection is afforded, availability of state coverage depresses the maximum.

There is some indication that the two- to four-month range for a maternity leave is the overwhelmingly dominant pattern in the states with their own statutory provision (75 percent of our respondents in these states in contrast to 51 percent in other states). However, only 19 percent of companies offer more than four months in these states (all offering six months) in contrast to 40 percent elsewhere (with no precise distribution pattern).

By themselves, then, state-level benefits provide minimum coverage, especially important for women working at low or median wages in firms without private insurance. In addition, the state benefit offers an opportunity for a public-private partnership in benefit provision, since private insurance can "top off" the state benefit for higher earning employees in firms with such coverage. Here, our evidence as to extent is limited, although we have case evidence. One could argue either that the same factors contributing to the development of state TDI have also influenced the development of private provision; or that the existence of statutory benefits stimulates the development of private provision; or some combination. In chapter 5 we explore how this interrelationship actually gets played out.

In any effort to account for statutory provision in these five states, attention should be paid to factors that might account for differences, such as the fact that female labor force participation rates are somewhat higher than in the rest of the country. In all except New York women represent a larger proportion of the labor force in these states than in the country as a whole. These are states that have tended to be more generous in social provisions than other states. Although all these factors warrant examination, we do not attempt it here.

In 1981, at least 20 percent of the private labor force was entitled to neither a paid sick leave nor disability insurance benefits at the time of maternity; 35 percent had sick leave benefits only. Including coverage provided through state TDI, where available, the best and most generous estimates we can make of the proportion of women working in the private sector who are entitled to a paid maternity leave beyond the basic minimum permitted through a paid sick leave is a little over 50 percent. Excluding state benefits, which at any rate provide very low benefits for women earning median wages or higher, the coverage, at best, is 48 percent. This is likely to be a substantial overestimate.

Since our data for states without TDI are biased away from small employers (those least likely to provide paid maternity leave), we would judge that in reality less than half, probably much less, have any such benefit coverage at all, and probably less than 40 percent are covered by their employers (see table 4.4). The one employee survey we have, the QES, found that 29 percent of the women working more than twenty hours per week had such coverage in 1977, but that this figure was 28 percent less than was indicated by employer surveys at that same time. (Of course, employees are often far less aware of their

**Table 4.4.** Estimating Coverage of Pregnancy and Maternity by Disability Insurance, 1981

|  | Calculations (millions) | Coverage (millions) |
|---|---|---|
| 1. Civilian labor force (employed) | 98.0 | |
| 2. Less government employees (16.2) = | 81.8 | |
| Labor force in states with TDI (21.1) less government employees (3.5) = | 17.6 | |
| Coverage rate for 5 states @ 82% | | 14.4 |
| Private labor force in states without TDI (81.9 − 17.6) = | 64.3 | |
| Less self-employed and unpaid family labor (7.7) = | 56.6 | |
| Coverage rate @ 48% | | 27.2 |
| | | 41.6 = 50.8% |

NOTE: As indicated in the text, these calculations require correction for the fact that female workers are concentrated in lower-coverage establishments.

entitlements than employers, especially concerning a benefit that has no immediate relevance.) Although our employer data are better than what have been available earlier, we caution that they are still possibly flawed in the indicated ways. Furthermore, for those employees entitled to state benefits only, benefit levels everywhere but California are very low.

Even for those fortunate enough to be protected by paid maternity leaves through disability insurance, six to eight weeks is the prevailing maximum. Few women are entitled to any longer for a normal pregnancy and delivery. Unpaid, but job-protected leaves are generally available, but these offer no real economic protection. Some women may supplement these benefits with vacation time. Others may be forced to use vacation time and sick leave just to gain even a modicum of paid leave.

Although basic health insurance seems available to most women employees, a significant proportion of women, especially young women and single (divorced) women—the group most in need—have no such coverage. These than are the data from existing surveys and reports. We turn in the next chapter to a picture of how these policies operate in real-life situations.

# 5. MATERNITY POLICIES IN PRIVATE INDUSTRY: THE OPERATING PICTURE

Chapter 1 began with specific people, then we turned to numbers dealing with larger aggregates. Now we translate those numbers and policies to the level of some specific firms, and to the experiences of their employees, supervisors, and managers.

Recall first some of the main features of the overall picture.

More than 90 percent of the respondents to our 1981 survey provide health and medical insurance coverage for pregnancy and maternity; 88 percent permit maternity leaves; 72 percent guarantee the same or a comparable job upon return to work. Of our survey respondent firms, 66 percent provide a paid sick leave, usually quite brief for employees with short terms of service; 48 percent provide short-term disability insurance. The typical duration of such benefits for a normal pregnancy is 6 weeks. Many allow subsequent unpaid personal leaves as well, often without job protection after an initial period.

However, there are significant variations across state lines, as the discussion of temporary disability insurance in the previous chapter indicates. At any one time, relatively few working women are using these benefits; but most of those who do are back at work, at the same job, within six months of childbirth, if not well before that.

These data cover both middle-size and larger companies, and they prove to be in many ways alike in what they offer. Smaller businesses, we know, are likely to provide far less—indeed very little—in the way of formal policies, guarantees, and benefits. While some smaller companies are included in our account, the information we summarize is skewed toward those with more generous provision.

In any case, data about aggregates may mask range and diversity, providing little sense of process and dynamics. We therefore turn now to a picture of how these policies are carried out "on the ground." How are they implemented in fact, not just in theory? What is the operating picture from the perspective of employees who qualify for and use the benefit, of supervisors and managers who administer it, of employers who pay for it, and of the society at large concerned with questions of equity, adequacy, efficiency?

From what has been said it follows that our cases are not and could not be—in number and method of selection—a random sample of the universe of private employers. We visited fifteen companies that were specifically selected to represent large and medium-sized companies that could be expected to provide relatively generous benefits and a range of industries, geographic locations, and types of employees.

The companies vary in size from 500 to 80,000 employees, from labor force composition of about one-third to more than two-thirds female, from agriculture to manufacturing, to high technology and service industries, and in locations from the east to the west coast.

In addition to the printed material each company makes available on its benefit plans and its related employee policies and practices, our information comes from interviews with human resource officers, front-line supervisors, and employees who themselves had experienced what it was like to become pregnant while working.

We make no claim about the complete generalizability of the picture we offer here. Our purpose is to report the diversity, the limitations, and problems of what is available even if one looks at the more generous employers. If they are the models, what can we expect as the future directions of the rest?

## HEALTH INSURANCE

All the firms we visited provide group health and medical insurance for their employees. However, there is enormous range in the extensiveness and adequacy of coverage, in the cost to employees, and in employees' understanding of what is and what is not available to them.

For one matter, not every company provides major medical insurance benefits; and even among those who do, maximum lifetime coverage ranges from $20,000 to $1 million. Moreover, hospital charges covered go from a maximum of $100 per day to all "usual and customary charges and fees," and allowable doctors' fees vary similarly. This is not the place for a full discussion of health insurance coverage in private industry, yet the range in the quality of coverage, even for what pertains to maternity and pregnancy, is astonishing.

The importance of the health insurance benefit was stressed everywhere, by employees and employers alike. Given the growing concern among employers with rising costs of health insurance, we were not surprised to hear human resource staff discussing proposals for controlling health insurance costs. Yet without exception, all emphasized the importance of this benefit and indicated that for young workers it is probably the single most important nonwage benefit they receive. Employees responded similarly, indicating that assurance of adequate health insurance coverage for their families was an important element in job decisions.

The importance of such benefit coverage for female employees was stressed by those who were themselves single parents, those whose husbands were self-employed, and those whose husbands were unemployed. One woman told us:

My husband lost his job soon after I became pregnant. It took him six months before he got another one, and I would not have been covered under his company's plan for this pregnancy. We were so worried about money. His unemployment benefits couldn't make up for his paycheck and you have no health insurance when you are unemployed. I was so relieved knowing that I—and the baby—were fully covered.

Another, explaining why maternity leaves represented such a forward step for a working woman, said: "It's not only that your job is saved for you. It's that they keep the health insurance up too. A lot of women will only stay out as long as they get their benefits covered, especially health insurance. If the family's protection depends on you, you don't want to lose it. It is worth too much."

Most employers we visited provide whatever it is they offer in the way of health insurance without requiring any contribution by employees to meeting the costs of the benefit. As indicated, the benefit levels may and do vary enormously, but where this benefit is fully paid by the employer, employees are assured of a defined minimum of coverage. However, where employees are required to pay for health insurance themselves in whole or in part, or to pay for certain "extra" coverage such as maternity, or to pay for dependents' coverage, these benefits may seem like costly options to a low-wage employee. Often, they forego the benefit. Sometimes this is a sensible decision—if, for example, a spouse has similar or even better coverage and the employee's coverage would be redundant.

For many employees who forego health insurance, however, this may not be the situation. Instead, the issue may be cost to a person with a marginal income, or even ignorance. "I was living at home and thought that my father's insurance covered me," said one young woman. "I never thought I'd get sick or anything, and why waste the money?" Instead she got pregnant and had an abortion, but none of her expenses was covered, and she had to borrow money to pay her bills. "I thought my husband's job covered us, so I never signed up for anything. When I got pregnant, I discovered that his company's plan only covered him, not me and a baby," was another woman's plaintive comment.

Some employees have learned that apparent benefit redundancy, where husbands and wives are both employed but with different companies, may in fact not be quite that. In one large company that wants to be competitive but not "state of the art," in its benefits, lower-level office employees have a medical-hospital plan that, essentially, pays the obstetrician up to about

$600 at the point of delivery and reimburses 80 percent of hospital charges (semiprivate accommodations) after a small deductible. Actual doctor fees for women who had recently had babies or were expecting them within a few months ranged from $600 to $1,200. A number of these women had husbands with medical coverage elsewhere, under which they were included as dependents. For them, the second policy served as coinsurance and met the 20 percent uncovered portion, also supplementing the doctor fees. They were grateful. Yet those without husbands or with husbands who did not have coverage for them faced a fee that, while manageable, was significant.

It is, then, not sufficient to find out whether a firm offers health insurance. The details of coverage may mean vastly different levels of protection, and the value of this protection is dependent on the employees' understanding of the often complicated provisions.

Policy implementation is a central issue here. The quality of benefit administration is not quite as important as benefit adequacy, but it is noteworthy. The importance of information and good communication concerning health insurance as well as other benefits is underscored by the comments of two women who worked in different companies. The first company is among the largest in the country, with a rich and comprehensive benefit package. The second is much smaller with rather modest benefits. The generosity of the benefit was not the issue. An employee of the first company complained bitterly about how no one had told her she would not have maternity coverage unless she elected the contributory disability benefit: "You only qualify for maternity coverage after six months of work and you must specifically ask for it." She became pregnant after two years on the job, and when she gave birth, discovered that she had no coverage at all.

In contrast, the employee at the second company told us how the personnel officer had called her in personally as soon as she heard about the pregnancy to advise her about adding on dependent's coverage that would cover her baby also. The woman gave birth prematurely and the baby had to remain in the hospital several weeks. All the expenses were covered by her insurance. She was thoroughly and appropriately convinced that without the advice of the company's personnel office, she would not have understood the implications of dependent's coverage and might not have known to ask for it.

Finally, although all the somewhat older women we spoke to talked of how much better health insurance policies are than in earlier years, several spoke of a desire for "well baby" coverage: some way whereby health insurance could cover routine preventive medical checkups for children and the immunization program in their early years. Basic pediatric checkups and routine visits for maternal and child health care still remain an uncovered basic health expenditure for most women as employees or as dependents despite the growth in group health insurance plan coverage at the workplace and the expansion in public coverage of "well baby" care for the very poor until the early 1980s.

## UNPAID MATERNITY LEAVES

All the firms we studied permit some kind of maternity leave at the time of a normal childbirth. Sometimes specifically labeled maternity leave but often as part of something called personal leave (and in one place an anticipated disability leave), the variations have to do with when the leave starts, how long it lasts, whether jobs are guaranteed upon return to work, whether benefits are protected and to what extent, and, of course, what portion of the leaves are paid. The portion of the leave that is paid and the means of payment are discussed subsequently. Here we explore the different patterns of unpaid leaves.

We note, parenthetically, that our use of the term maternity rather than parental does not stem from lack of appreciation of the measures in a few countries and a few unusual U.S. companies to permit fathers to participate in post-childbirth child care. We found such parental leave to be rare in American firms.

The briefest maternity leave we encountered is provided by a leading heavy manufacturing company with about 20,000 employees, largely male and largely unionized. The leave is limited to whatever period the woman employee is diagnosed as disabled. The longest leave is provided by a leading utility company with about 80,000 employees, largely female and also extensively unionized. There a personal leave of twelve months is permitted theoretically, but since the job is guaranteed only for a maximum of six months, most employees view the leave as really limited to the shorter period. Clearly this latter firm is still among the "generous" elite.

One firm permits a thirty-day personal leave on top of a disability leave that usually is six weeks but ranges up to twelve weeks. Even though employees at this firm may also add on vacation time if they wish, the typical overall leave in this, as in all but one other company visited, is two to three months. Three companies limit the leave permitted to the time the woman is diagnosed as disabled. But the strictness with which this diagnosis is made varies sufficiently so that in one firm women return within four to six weeks after childbirth while in others they are out eight to ten weeks on average. Most firms separate the unpaid and paid leaves; yet except for the company mentioned earlier, the average time women workers are out on leave is consistently reported as "between two and three months," including both paid and unpaid leaves. This figure is consistent with our survey data: more than two-thirds of the firms with a specified maximum leave indicated that it was three months or less.

For the most part, what is reported is a post-childbirth leave. Most female employees seem to be working up until the last minute of their pregnancy—often going into labor from work; or at most they stop working a week or two before they expect to give birth. This is in very sharp contrast to the pattern in the early 1970s and before, when women were often required to stop working six weeks before their baby was due, no matter what they preferred.

Only where women have physically demanding jobs are they likely to begin their leaves well before childbirth. Some companies will change a woman's job for a few months if her work is hazardous, and firms in hazardous industries tend to define the onset of disability earlier. At one company, most pregnant women who are farm field and shed workers leave work in their seventh month and qualify for statutory disability benefits at that point. In another industry, at a firm with private disability insurance, we were told that the lack of consistency in the way disability is diagnosed and defined within the company was a major problem in its efforts to administer maternity policies. Even within the same plant, one pregnant woman may be assigned to a lighter job, and discharged if she refuses it, while a second may be diagnosed as disabled and permitted to go on leave.

Firms routinely follow circuitous paths just to administer their basic policies. One firm, for example, permits employees to take personal leave some days or weeks prior to childbirth and then, through a device whereby the employee shifts back to employment status for one day, the woman qualifies for sickness or disability leave beginning at the time of actual delivery. Moreover, the employee is then also permitted to transfer back again to qualify for a brief subsequent period of personal leave once no longer considered by the doctor as disabled by pregnancy and maternity. The purpose of this shifting back and forth has to do with such fundamental issues as job protection, pay, and benefit coverage. This is a firm that permits a three-month personal leave and also allows employees to remain participants in various insurance plans (health, life) only for a maximum of three months, and even then only if the employee contributes. However, the temporary disability leave assures the employee of both pay and benefits, a not insignificant amount of compensation. The result is, of course, that employees try to maximize the period they are defined as disabled.

Another firm distinguishes between those employees who go on leave before giving birth, taking advantage of an anticipated disability leave, and those who begin their leave only when they go into labor or who take their vacation benefit near the end of their pregnancy and go into labor while they are on vacation. The distinction between whether an individual is on the anticipated disability leave or the sickness-disability leave associated with delivery is tied to whether the employee must pay for her own health insurance (yes, if on anticipated disability) and how the leave is assessed for purposes of tracking absenteeism (she is marked absent if claiming sickness-disability). Although the distinction seems clear-cut to management, it is not to employees and, as a consequence, confusion and resentment are common.

One young woman told us how she gave birth prematurely while on vacation, and the problems she and her husband faced when trying to clarify what she was entitled to. Another said she would have scheduled her vacation differently if she had known she would be classified as absent-sick while on maternity (anticipated disability) leave.

An insurance company permits an eighteen-week leave specifically for maternity purposes. Although in theory this is a maximum leave, employees view it as an automatic entitlement. In addition, they are entitled to up to ten days unpaid personal leave per year which can be used if needed to care for an ill child. (We return to this subject subsequently.)

While most companies have a single companywide policy, this isn't always the case. A high technology and heavy manufacturing company has benefits and maternity policies that vary significantly across divisions. The high tech division permits a six-month maternity leave (in contrast to three months for all other personal leaves) but only provides a job guarantee for the first four months of that leave. Since the labor market is tight for such companies, the reality is that employees who want to return can, in fact, do so. By contrast, at its headquarters office, no personal leave policy exists and women employees, entitled only to a disability leave, must return to work immediately upon recovery as defined by the doctor, if they wish to stay with the firm.

## Ambiguities and Inconsistencies in Leave Policies

Our interviews convince us that there is considerable confusion and disagreement over whether employers are still permitted under federal law to establish special maternity policies or whether all leaves, sickness, and disability policies must be general, stated, and implemented in a form that applies equally to disability and illness conditions that could affect any male or female employees. At least one human resource officer stated that women have lost out at his firm as a consequence of the

1978 legislation because the company used to permit a six-month unpaid leave for maternity and now, out of fear that men would claim it too, for other disabilities, limits the leave to the period of disability without specifying the amount of time. Most leaves are briefer as a result. Despite this interpretation, about half of the companies we studied have explicitly labeled maternity policies and, indeed, often permit more generous leaves connected with maternity reasons than for other purposes. (Of course the long-term disability policy, dealing with conditions that go beyond six months and can often be lifelong, are another matter.)

The lack of consistency in the meaning of a maternity leave or a personal leave is dramatized in the range of policies on job security for employees on leave. Some firms guarantee the same or a comparable job, but the definition of comparability varies widely. At companies having a large number of outlets, the definition of a comparable job may include a different but geographically related store or restaurant. Some companies do not guarantee the same job but say that turnover is so high that employees are likely to get a similar job back if they wish it. Other firms state that if the employee is out only a brief time, the job will be held but not beyond a specified maximum (four weeks; six weeks; sixty days; six months). Often the job guarantee time is shorter than the maximum unpaid leave that is permitted. State temporary disability legislation does not always require that a job be held for an employee; the only requirement is that the company policy be the same for all employees in the same firm or state.

There is similar inconsistency in whether or not employees are entitled to benefit coverage while on leave. Some firms continue such coverage throughout the leave, some for a specified period only. Some continue coverage for the employee but require the worker to pay for dependents' coverage; some permit the employee to contribute while on leave in order to continue benefits normally paid for by the employer. And some firms sharply limit even the employee's entitlement to participate in the group plan, not offering the option of paying the contribution.

In some firms, the protection of seniority rights may be an

issue. In a company where seniority carries with it the right to preferred tasks, or even a priority for a job (not a guarantee of one), the period of time for which seniority is protected becomes an important issue in the company's maternity policy.

Each of these constraints—job protection, seniority protection, and benefit protection—is a critical aspect of a maternity leave and plays an important role, along with the overriding issue of wage replacement, in the employee's decision about the length of the leave she will take.

One woman told us:

> I planned on taking off a year. He was my first and it had taken eight years before I got pregnant. A first child is always very special and this one was even more so. My pregnancy was easy and I took my vacation beginning in my eighth month. He was born early, while I was still on vacation, and they put me on sick leave. I knew I would only be paid for my six weeks, but we had scrimped and saved and I was determined to stay home with him that first year. Two weeks before he was six months old, they called me and said if I wanted to keep my job I would have to be back at work in two weeks. I couldn't believe it. The book says you can take a twelve-month maternity leave. They told me that my job would be kept only for six months. I had worked for the company for fifteen years, and I thought they owed me something more for that period. My pension was almost vested. I needed the health insurance but was paying for the benefits. My husband had been out of work once for six months and I couldn't take that chance again. I was afraid to lose my job. So I went back, but I didn't want to.

Other women told similar stories.

> I stayed out for three months even though I got paid only for four weeks. I would have stayed out longer, but you lose your health benefits if you are out longer, and with a new baby I could not afford that.

> People talk about maternity leaves. There's no real leave. You barely get over having the baby when you have to go back to work. My doctor said stay out six weeks, eight weeks, but my boss kept saying "How long does it take to get over having a baby?" In four weeks you should be back at work.

They told me that they couldn't give me my same job, but they would give me a job in the store across town. They said it was almost the same because the job was the same, just in a different place. But it's not the same. It takes me another half hour to get there, and I have to change buses twice. When I worked at the other place, I could go to my sister's during my lunch hour. That would let me visit with the baby. The manager is different too. If I am a few minutes late he complains, but it is hard to tell when the bus will come and how long it will take. It doesn't matter what they say, I wish I had my old job back. This one is not the same. My old boss said he would let me know if someone leaves so I can go back.

Some women get their jobs back and some find that the comparable job is acceptable. Some return to work very soon and are happy about it: some return after four weeks and some after two or three. Stories are told about women who work until the day they go into labor. One report was of a woman who worked right up to the last moment on a Friday and gave birth that evening. By Monday she was back at her desk. (Fortunately, her supervisor sent her home.)

Women executives and professionals are often on the phone within a few hours after giving birth. Some with more flexible schedules talk of organizing their work so that they go into their office for a few hours at a time and then for a half day or a day a week, taking work home with them and then gradually making a transition from home to work. Most such women are away from work only briefly. Four to six weeks may be all they want or need. Moreover, if they need or want more time, they usually have the right to flexibility and to use their own judgment in taking more.

These women, however, should not be seen as common, nor as a general model. For the great majority of women without such flexibility and autonomy and the income with which to buy needed help, the constraints on maternity leave still seem stringent. This is especially true for those who would prefer to be home longer and can eke out the money to do so but cannot afford loss of job protection.

Our conclusion, after studying how policies are implemented in a number of firms among those usually viewed as having generous benefits, is that it is not yet clear what a job-protected maternity leave really is since jobs are not fully protected, nor are benefits, nor is seniority beyond a very limited period. And even where there is such protection, two to three months is the norm. Some of the very large firms insist that their leave policies were more generous before the 1978 legislation. They claim that now concern about possible allegations of discrimination has constrained their freedom to provide more generous leaves at the time of maternity. Yet, as we have seen, several employers do treat maternity more generously than other conditions. Regardless, where leaves are available, they are not truly comparable across firms in any way. The length seems to be beginning to be standardized, but there is not much else in the way of protection.

Now we turn to what some view as the central issue of maternity policies: what portion of this leave is paid and how?

## PAID LEAVES

Paid maternity leaves began to be available on a formal basis in the 1970s. Initially, most of these leaves involved very brief paid periods as part of sick leave. No firm responding to our mail survey has a special maternity income plan any longer. Such leaves are paid for today out of sickness benefits, vacation pay, short-term or long-term disability benefits, some kind of salary continuation plan (especially for managers and executives), or some combination of these. The amount of pay a working woman on maternity leave may receive and the length of time she can receive it could therefore depend upon the type of plan from which her benefits are paid (sickness, short-term or long-term disability, salary continuation, etc.), the length of time she has worked for the firm, where she lives and works, the extent of her disability before and after childbirth, as stated by her doctor, and, of course, her wage or salary level.

### Type of Plan

Both the maximum weekly benefit and the maximum number of weeks the benefit can be paid are determined by the type of plan under which the benefit is provided. For most employees, the right to receive pay at the time of maternity depends on whether or not they have a right to a paid sick leave. Indeed, as we have stressed, for a substantial proportion of the work force, sickness benefits alone, or perhaps in conjunction with vacation benefits, constitute an employee's sole protection against income loss at the time of childbirth. In many cases, especially for employees with relatively brief periods of service, sickness benefits may mean the right to only two weeks pay when away from work because of illness, and then often only at half pay.

Although employees who have worked for a firm for a longer time usually have a longer benefit entitlement and at a higher level of payment, very few sickness benefit plans permit longer than four weeks and often then only through the right to accrue or accumulate unused sick leave, up to a specified maximum. This is a slow process. In many companies employees accrue sick leave at the rate of one week per year.

For young women employees, the right to a four-week leave may mean no—or almost no—use of sick leave for four or five years. Moreover, the use of all sickness benefits at the time of maternity may eliminate any entitlement to such benefits during the first year after childbirth. This can be even more of a problem if the employee has, as may be the case, "borrowed" against future benefits.

Furthermore, the label of sickness attached to the maternity benefit may carry stigma or penalty even though all concerned know that pregnancy and childbirth are not an illness and should not be viewed in the same light. An employee may find herself listed as out "ill" above average, even if she has seldom used sick leave before. Only a legislative or legalistic artifact requires that the label of sickness or disability be applied to pregnancy and maternity if there is to be income protection at that time.

A single mother who worked as a cashier at a coffee shop said:

I had two weeks sick leave, and he let me add my two weeks vacation to that, so I was out for four weeks all together. I'm on my feet a lot so I wanted to take more time off, but I couldn't afford to be out without getting paid. They were pretty decent about it and let me use a high stool so I could sit part of the time.

In contrast, another single mother in a similar situation, but working for a national restaurant chain, said that as long as her combined sick leave and vacation benefits covered her for four weeks she was "home free" because the company's long-term disability plan went into effect then.

Even though I didn't get my full wage, it was just about the same as my take-home pay, and it is tax free. Since I wait on tables and am on my feet almost the whole time, my doctor said I had to be out for six weeks after I gave birth. I was out all together for two and one half months, from the beginning of my ninth month until the baby was six weeks old, all paid for. Of course, I lost my tips.

Still another mother reported that the leave, while paid for, created unforeseen and unanticipated problems because she had received what was technically a sickness benefit.

I had worked for the company for fifteen years when I had my baby. Everybody always talked about what great benefits the company has, and it does, but not for maternity. I took as much time off as I could—six months—even though I knew there was no way the whole time would be paid for. I had three weeks vacation time coming to me and I left in the middle of my ninth month. I got five weeks sickness and disability pay after the baby was born, took the rest of what was owed me for vacation and the remainder as personal leave. My husband and I had figured out that we could manage without my paycheck for four months, so we agreed I would take six months off. But nobody told me that if I took time off for the baby, it would be counted as if I was really sick! When I got back to work, they put my name on the list of people who had a high absentee rate. That meant if I was sick anymore for the next year, I could be fired. The baby was sick a lot that first year, and I was up a lot at night. I was tired all the time and kept getting colds. When I got colds, the baby got colds too. And when he got sick, I got sick. My doctor told me I was run down and needed to be home for a few days. But I couldn't do it. I was afraid I would lose my job and we couldn't afford that. Can you imagine that? After fifteen years of working for a company with only a few days off for sickness during that whole time—and I take off for maternity, and they mark me as someone who is sick a lot. It's crazy to consider maternity the same as a virus infection.

For those employees covered by short-term (or short-term and long-term) disability benefits, the availability of a paid leave, the benefit level, and the duration of the benefit are more consistent. Most find that six to eight weeks is the typical period covered (two weeks before birth and six weeks after) under the rubric of disability for a normal pregnancy and delivery. A Caesarean delivery usually means another two weeks of coverage. A young woman with a complicated pregnancy or complications on delivery may receive a substantial cash benefit, representing a larger proportion of her wages (than does the alternative sickness pay) for as long as twenty-six weeks under short-term disability insurance, or longer if she is covered under a long-term disability plan.

One young woman told us how she became pregnant after working for a company for a year and a half, knowing nothing of her company's benefits for pregnant women. Once she discovered what kind of coverage she had, she expected to work until her ninth month, take her vacation then, and receive whatever temporary disability leave she was entitled to. Her plan was to be back at work when the baby was about a month old. Instead, in the middle of her pregnancy toxemia set in. She was hospitalized for six weeks and then sent home to convalesce. After childbirth she was hospitalized again because of a blood clot in her leg. All in all she was away from her job for six months and was paid a good part of her wages for that whole period. Few are so happily surprised, though ignorance of coverage appears widespread.

## Length of Service

How long an employee has worked for a firm has immediate consequences for the maximum duration of the benefit, especially if the maternity leave pay is made up of sickness benefits, or sickness and vacation benefits combined. Without exception among the companies we studied, employees are entitled to receive such benefits only after working for at least six months. Usually they are entitled to a maximum of a week of sick pay only after one year. Even if they are permitted to accumulate unused sick leave, it is rare that an employer will permit an accrual of more than four weeks (after that, some employers "cash out" some proportion of the leave's value). This usually means that if one depends on sickness benefits for maternity coverage, only after about five years service—and minor use of sick leave—will a working woman have the right to a four-week paid leave, which, when coupled with the standard two-week vacation, would permit a six-week maternity leave at full pay.

The situation is somewhat better under short-term or long-term disability. Once the requirements of public statutory coverage or private insurance coverage are met, the duration is more generous than the sick leave. Full achievement of coverage is almost everywhere completed during a first year of employment at most.

However, length of service also may affect the benefit levels under both sickness and disability plans. Thus, for example, in several of the firms studied, an employee who had worked for her firm for less than two years out on sick leave or disability leave would receive half pay only. Typically a woman who has worked for an employer for two to five years would be entitled to four weeks full pay and then half pay (up to one year if the disability warranted this) and to thirteen weeks of full pay if she had worked for the firm for five years or more. Despite these stated maxima, it must be remembered that actual coverage for a normal pregnancy and delivery is limited to the period of time a woman is viewed as disabled. Again, prevailing practice is to define this as a period of six to eight weeks in toto, including six weeks after birth.

## Place of Residence and Work

Geography plays an important role in determining whether a working woman receives any paid benefit at the time of maternity, as well as how much the benefit is. As we indicated in the last chapter, five states provide or mandate statutory temporary disability insurance that covers pregnancy and maternity as well as all other nonwork-related disabilities. For women working for small employers, especially employers who provide no private insurance coverage, and for women working at unskilled, low-wage jobs, such coverage is enormously important. Surprisingly enough, state TDI benefits represent important supplementary coverage too, even among the large firms offering good short-term disability insurance themselves.

California, the state with the most generous TDI benefits, is an excellent illustration of both types of advantages. Agricultural workers, for example, who are unlikely to be covered under private insurance, are covered nonetheless under the state benefit plan. Where there is some entitlement to a personal leave, even if all that is protected is the seniority and the right to be called up to work ahead of others, the state TDI benefit assures partial wage replacement. For those who work for firms with excellent private insurance benefits, the state plan may permit an even more generous benefit package to be put together.

One personnel manager in a state with TDI explained to us the principle guiding her company's approach to protecting employees' interests. She stressed that her company's policy toward maternity as well as all other illnesses or short-term disabilities is "to help employees maximize their benefit entitlement so that they can get a full wage package." Thus, those employees who are receiving the state disability benefit, which at the time of our study paid a maximum of $154 per month, may receive both sickness pay and vacation pay to top off the state benefit or the private insurance benefit (if the company provides it) and reach full wage replacement. When an employee files for the state benefit, she is permitted to report that she has no salary. The sickness benefit paid by the company is then added to the state benefit, to create a full wage replacement.

A typical employee's combined benefit package in this company may include the state disability benefit, a sickness benefit equal to two days pay per week, and if necessary even some vacation benefit time added on at the end. However, in this instance, the state benefit component is used only for the first four weeks of what is usually a six-week leave, because after four weeks the company's long-term disability insurance plan goes into effect. Although this benefit provides only a 60 percent wage replacement (up to a specified maximum amount, as is characteristic of all plans, short and long term, private and statutory), that is also higher than what would be available through the state. Since it, too, is tax free, however, it does mean that the net pay, for a substantial proportion of employees, is well protected. Of particular interest, given our concern with the young women employees who are likely to become pregnant, an average employee who has worked for the company for at least one year would be able to get the equivalent of her full salary for six weeks with this policy.

California women employees are an advantaged group at the time of maternity. Firms operating in several states, including states with and states without such coverage, are aware of the inequities that exist as a consequence. Indeed, some companies whose private insurance plans are predicated on the existence of the state benefit, may find themselves in a peculiar position in another state having no TDI. In one instance, a firm having only a basic, brief sick leave benefit and a long-term disability plan that goes into effect only after an employee has been with the firm at least two years informally decided to adjust its eligibility requirements for employees in other states to match the states with mandatory benefits. Their company's plan now offers young women some protection at the time of maternity in all states. Since they are self-insurers, they look the other way when employees with less than two years' service become pregnant and cover them with long-term disability benefits for which they are technically not eligible. Thus, with some minimum entitlement to sick leave and vacation pay (three weeks combined), a young woman who works for this firm would have coverage for all but about one of the six weeks of maternity leave. Recognize, however, that this generosity is dependent on complicated procedures that involve informal rule-breaking—hardly a general model for the private sector.

## The Length of the Leave: The Extent of the Disability

As we mentioned earlier, only the availability of statutory or private disability insurance assures many women employees of even six to eight weeks of paid leave. Under some circumstances, the length of paid leave may be extended to ten weeks for a normal pregnancy and delivery. Despite the presence of disability insurance, and regardless of the level at which the benefit is paid, or whether the employees benefiting are exempt and or nonexempt, *we have found no firm and no state that provides a paid leave for more than twelve weeks at the maximum, including time before and after normal childbirth.* To be sure, in some places, this maximum may be supplemented by vacation time and pay, and pregnancy and birth complications are excluded from this generalization; but these considerations are largely irrelevant in specifying the routine length of leave.

In effect, even under the most generous provision, available only to a small proportion of the female labor force, paid maternity leaves in U.S. companies are limited to less time than the briefest statutory leave in Europe and in all other advanced industrial countries. The reason for this is that the length of the leave is limited to that period of time physicians diagnose their pregnant or postpartum patients as disabled.

As several company human resources officers argued, the very large and leading companies were gradually moving toward providing more generous maternity benefits for their female employees. But, they further claimed, after the 1978 legislation defined pregnancy as a disability subject to the same protection as other disabilities, these companies reassessed their policies. If maternity is a disability, so their argument goes, it must be treated like all others. It was necessary to limit the benefit or they would be required to treat all disabilities of men or women more generously. They hold that it is beside the point to argue that before 1978 most employees did not have the right to paid maternity leave: "We had already established more generous policies for unpaid maternity leaves and would have moved this way for paid leaves, too," we were told. Whether or not this would have happened is irrelevant now. Representatives of the big and forward-thinking companies usually acknowledge that, in any case, small, medium-sized, or less progressive companies were unlikely to move toward paid leaves without direct prodding by government. Regardless, the federal legislation was passed, and employers have extended coverage of paid leaves to a larger portion of the female labor force, even though how much larger is still difficult to ascertain because of the paucity of precise earlier data and problems with current data.

Given the criterion of disability and related incapacity to work as the measure for the paid leave, the result is at best a very brief leave. Both the very medical advances that have increasingly defined pregnancy and childbirth as normal conditions, requiring only a brief convalescence, and the antidiscrimination measures that have insisted that women not be disqualified from work unless physically unable to carry on have spurred the shortening of the period women are viewed as disabled. Paradoxically enough, they have therefore restricted even further the economically protected maternity leave. The insecurities of leave policies are still further exacerbated by the lack of any firm agreement as to the period of time the woman will be defined as disabled at the time of a normal pregnancy and maternity.

Nonetheless, an understandable and readily explainable variation exists for the pre-childbirth component of a paid leave. As noted, among the firms studied, almost all permit a woman to work to the last moment if she wishes and if her doctor concurs. Many women do stop work at some point during their ninth month of pregnancy. Those who leave earlier are usually those who are engaged in demanding physical work. If the employer can provide a temporary alternative in the form of a less demanding job, the woman may continue to work until the time that most such women generally leave work. If the industry is such that no such alternative is possible (in some forms of agricultural work, for example), she is likely to be diagnosed as disabled earlier and thus eligible to stop work and receive benefits. Even in such cases, there are often disagreements and variations in policies across and within firms.

Although the pattern for post-childbirth paid leave is far more consistent—a standard six weeks is prevailing practice—this varies too. In one company, the policy requires approval of the disability period by a company physician. The company's own medical policy is that a four-week leave is all that is warranted after normal childbirth. The consequence is that women employees who are informed and sophisticated, and know this, discuss it with their own physicians who often explicitly indicate a six- or eight-week convalescence as essential. These women refuse to return to work earlier, refusing even to come to the company's clinic for a check-up. The result is that they usually do get paid for the full six to eight weeks as proposed by their own physicians. Other employees, who may be less knowledgeable about their company's practices—or less assertive—get penalized. They may take the time off but do not receive the pay and indeed may be pressured to return to work before they are really ready to or want to.

The following two case stories are from this large company with many female employees, which has its own medical department:

I expected to be home for three months. I really wanted to, but then my husband lost his job. The unemployment benefits were not enough, so I had to come back sooner. But I was sure I would have six weeks paid for. My doctor wrote on my form that I should come back to him for a check-up after four weeks. The company doctor told me that that meant I was able to return to work. The company doctor said that they would not pay me if I took off the other two weeks. I couldn't afford to be without pay then, so I went back to work even though I was still tired and weak. When my doctor heard, he got angry and said he would never have asked me to come back for a check-up then if he had understood the consequences.

They called me to come in for a check-up four weeks after I gave birth. I was staying at my mother's so she could help me with the baby, and it would have meant a one and a half hour car trip if I had to go to the company doctor for the check-up. My doctor told me not to, and I had a fight over the telephone with the company doctor. He said they wouldn't pay me, but I said I couldn't come in and my doctor had told me not to. They finally paid me for those two weeks. I told another girl in my department, "Don't let them browbeat you. Stand up for yourself and you are O.K." If I had gone for a check-up that time, they would have told me the same thing they told others: If you can come in for a check-up, you are well enough to go back to work.

## OTHER ISSUES: THE EMPLOYEE EXPERIENCE AND PERSPECTIVE

### An Exempt Employee's Perspective

Most of what we have described characterizes provision for nonexempt employees: those blue, pink, and white-collar workers who receive overtime pay if they work more than an eight-hour day or a forty-hour week. Generally speaking, exempt employees are treated more generously as to benefits, especially benefit levels and duration. When out on maternity leave, their salaries are usually fully covered under some kind of salary continuation plan. If, however, they too depend on disability insurance, the benefit duration is quite similar. In short, for most exempt employees the time for which they may receive salaries when out because of maternity also tends to be six to eight weeks. However, many exempt employees have more flexibility and often more autonomy. Thus, they may even begin to work sooner after childbirth but not return to full-time work until later.

We spoke with a young assistant manager in the trust department of a bank. She had worked for the company for ten years, was married, and had two children aged two and four. Her first maternity leave was taken in 1977. She took off four months at that time, a month before the baby was due and three months after. Four months was the company's standard disability leave even then, but it was all unpaid. Her second son was born at the end of July 1979, and she took off the same four months, but this time six weeks of the leave was fully paid.

During each of the leaves, I came into the office for one half-day each week for the first three months and then one day a week during the fourth month. From my perspective this was essential if I were to stay in touch with what was going on in the company, keep up somewhat with mail, phone calls, new developments, and manage an easy transition back to work at the end. If I were away for four months without any contact with the office, I would feel terribly unrelated when I got back. It could be a disaster. And can you imagine the mountain of work awaiting me on my return?"

She commented subsequently on how important the benefit was because it relieved her of some financial pressures. Similarly, she spoke of the advantages of flexibility—of coming to work a half day each week—because it permitted her to stay in touch with what was happening and to handle urgent matters. This ability, plus taking some work home that could be done there, relieved her of the tension that could build up if she had been away for a longer time without any regular contact. We were struck, though, by how many more options she had than her nonexempt counterparts on leave.

This same young woman said that she could not manage with less than four months' leave because she used a licensed child care center near her home to care for her children, and the program would only accept children from three months of age and up.

The child care option we preferred required that I be away from work at least three months. From what I have seen, the length of time a woman employee takes off after childbirth has to do with two factors: (1) the amount of financial pressure she is under, whether she can afford to be without her salary and if so, for how long; and (2) the kind of child care available to her. I am convinced that child care— the availability of good quality, reasonably priced, reliable child care— is often the most important factor in determining when a woman comes back to work.

This was from a woman who lives and works in a semirural community where it is generally assumed that most working women had plenty of family living nearby, able and willing to provide child care.

### Packaged Benefits and Fragmented Policies

For many women, the complicated amalgam of sickness benefits, vacation benefits, and disability benefits often means that during the pregnancy, childbirth, and postnatal period, they experience changing eligibility for health insurance, changes in whether they or their employers pay for the benefits, and a variety of other such changes with consequences for how they and their families are protected and at what cost.

I've had two children while working here. The oldest is three years old and the baby is nine months. You'd think the policies would be the same. They were both born after the 1978 legislation went into effect. But each leave was different and it made a difference to me. My first baby was born prematurely while I was on vacation. I immediately shifted to disability status when he was born. I kept all my benefits and the company paid for them. All the hospital and medical expenses for the baby were covered, and he had to stay in the hospital until he was five weeks old. It cost a fortune, but we didn't have to lay out a cent. When my second baby was due, the doctors decided that he might be a preemie too. I had taken my vacation earlier that year, so I asked for and was given a personal leave. The baby came earlier than the doctors expected and also had to stay in the hospital a while. This time, however, because I was on personal leave, my benefits were not covered, and I had to pay for them myself. Because I was in a panic about what might happen, we paid it, of course, but it was a terrible strain. If I had known that would happen and that I would have to pay the insurance myself, I would never have used my vacation time, but nobody told me.

In contrast, in another firm, if an employee takes a personal leave before childbirth, as soon as she is close to giving birth— or gives birth—her status is immediately changed back to an employment status for one day, so she can qualify for the full benefit coverage provided under the firm's disability insurance plan.

This type of fragmentation and maneuver is inevitable in the absence of adequate policy and provision.

## Information Giving and Receiving

As some of our cited interviews have already suggested, the amount of ignorance, misinformation, and confusion that exists among employees concerning their rights to pregnancy and childbirth benefits is truly huge. As one after another woman would say:

When I first came to work here and they told me about my benefits, I never paid any attention to anything said about maternity. I certainly never asked any questions. After all, I wasn't pregnant, and I wasn't planning on getting pregnant then, so what difference did it make to me? Only when I got pregnant myself did I begin to ask questions . . . and it's very hard to get decent answers. They say, "Here's a pamphlet on your benefits. Read it." But they are not easy to read and understand. When you ask people, you don't get straight answers. For example, nobody explains that it may make a difference whether you give birth while you are on vacation, or on personal leave, or on disability leave. And I didn't know that it mattered who decided how long I am disabled after childbirth. If my doctor says one thing and another doctor disagrees, who decides between them and how? Or, if my job isn't saved for me, what rights do I have? Or how long do they have to save it for me?

Moreover, because confusion, ignorance, and misinformation are so rampant, when employees turn to one another or their supervisors, the problem may get even worse.

My boss told me I had to come back to work or lose my job. I couldn't afford to lose my job so I came back even though I felt rotten and didn't want to. I got sick six weeks later and was out, and the doctor was furious when he heard I had gone back to work so soon. He called the company's personnel officer who said there was no reason for me to have returned to work then; my boss was wrong. But how was I to know that at the time?

Another woman in my department told me that you could stay out as long as you wanted to as long as you got your doctor to say you were disabled. I was nursing, so I wanted to stay out longer. My doctor put down twelve weeks, but then the insurance company wrote him and called him. They told me that all I would be paid for if I stayed out was five weeks. I had made no child care arrangements, and it meant that I would have to be back on the job in less than a week from then. My mother helped out, but she really hadn't planned to take care of him that soon. It was hard on the baby too, because I had to get him used to taking his bottle in the middle of the day when I wasn't there. If I had understood the way the policy worked, I could have planned better.

In a sense, the extent of ignorance may seem amazing, but it seems more the predictable outcome of a complex and at times irrational amalgamation of provisions that are poorly explained.

## Paternity, Adoption, and Part-Time Employees

As already noted, only two of the firms we studied permit paid paternity leaves, each for three or four days. The concept here is to permit a father to take time off when his wife gives birth, to help her when she arrives home with a new infant or, at the time of a second or subsequent childbirth, to take care of the child left at home. Although theoretically fathers could request personal leave to take care of a newborn—or share in the care of a baby—obviously this is not yet occurring very much.

On the other hand, several women employees told us that if their husband's employer permitted use of the employee's sick leave to care for an ill child at home, and their mother's employer did not, the fathers in these families were likely to take the time off and to provide the care.

Although several firms provide or plan to provide adoption benefits, all the adoption benefits discussed involve a subsidy for the costs surrounding adoption; none involves payment for a leave. Adoptive parents may be eligible for an unpaid personal leave, but since adoption is not a disabling condition, it carries with it no entitlement to a cash benefit. The tendency of the European maternity or parental leave plans to include the post-adoption period underscores the differences in concept.

Although some part-time employees have entitlements to health insurance and vacation benefits, in only one firm we studied are they covered by the maternity policies we have described here. Benefit coverage for part-time employees is a major problem and raises issues that go well beyond the maternity question.

### Employees' Response to Pregnancy and Childbirth

Most employees who took maternity leave at the companies we studied returned within six months after childbirth; and the general trend is for more employees to return each year, and to do so sooner.

There are variations, however, in how employees respond once they know they are pregnant, and these seem to reflect their ways of coping with company policy, or at least their perceptions of such policy. Most employees seem to announce they are pregnant as soon as they know and immediately request information about their entitlements, especially health insurance coverage and leaves. Some, who wish to keep their personal lives private or fear that their pregnancy will lead to some subtle form of discrimination in, for example, promotional opportunities, wait until their condition is obvious. Most employers have no special policies requiring that they be informed but urge employees to do so and to be sure that they are covered for all relevant benefits.

Some employees resign immediately at the time of childbirth even though they are entitled to a paid leave. They have decided to stop working and they want to define their status that way and not take a benefit that they are "not entitled to" despite the validity of their entitlement. Others leave at the end of their paid sickness or disability leave. If they have created the impression that they will return (technically the premise of all sickness and temporary-disability benefits), the company may be making do with temporary help or extra-work coverage by fellow workers. Lead time in recruitment is lost.

Several human resource officers emphasized, on the other hand, that employees who take their leave and then resign are not viewed as being unethical and are no different from employees who take their vacation and resign. It is an earned benefit. In one company we were told that some employees who do resign before taking a leave do so because they were given bad advice:

Our employee relations generalist should advise the employee to take the sick leave and then see how she feels—and whether she wants to resign. Some employees resign because they have decided not to work for a while and want to cash out any benefits they may have which will give them a lump sum cash entitlement when their baby is born.

The enlightened view seems to be that the employee should exercise her rights but let it be known that in fact she plans to resign. Many employers acknowledge, however, that current policies almost require a charade, whereby a woman employee announces a planned return, because otherwise she is viewed as resigning or quitting and, therefore, not qualifying for benefit protection.

## OTHER ISSUES: THE EMPLOYER'S AND THE MANAGER'S EXPERIENCE AND PERSPECTIVE

### Planning on Uncertainty

The major problem that maternity leaves and benefits present to employers is the need to ensure that the work is done while the employee is away. It often is necessary to make and carry out such plans without knowing whether the employee will return at the end of her leave. In explaining the problem, one human resource officer of a steel company said:

Here we are in a situation in which we are paying a substantial cash benefit for six weeks without any assurance that the employee will return to work. While she is out, her work has to be done. Either she will be replaced by a temporary worker or by someone else who will have to be trained. And until the last minute, there is no way to know whether or not she will return, even though far more, it is true, are coming back now than previously.

Sometimes it is different. Sometimes you know the employee is going to return. I have two secretaries in my department now on maternity leave, but I know they will come back.

When we questioned him as to how he could be so sure they would return, he responded,

Well, in one case the husband just lost his job and the woman's salary is essential for the family to survive. In the other case, the husband is going to college at night and is home during the day. He'll take care of the baby during the day because her salary is what they live on. And as each of these women are earning in the low twenties, they are not going to forego that income under the circumstances.

The director of the pension department in an insurance company acknowledged that although she understood the need to have leave for maternity reasons and appreciated that these benefits were important, there was a problem for those responsible for seeing that the work got done:

If you have complicated, responsible work that has to be done, the inability to make a plan with any degree of certainty is very frustrating. Furthermore, you are often terribly dependent on others carrying on well beyond their own jobs, and there are insufficient rewards for those who help out at such times. It is a serious problem when work cannot be paced and there are urgent time deadlines and scheduling problems. Take a look at my department, for example. There are 80 people in the department and twelve are out on maternity leave now. Although technically, four months is the maximum maternity leave allowed, that has become a standard, and most women take the four months even if they get paid only for six weeks, unless they are under severe financial pressures.

Given fifteen percent of my staff out on maternity leave for four months, at one time, it's very hard to get work out. We hire temporaries for routine work, but most of the work is not routine. It is impossible to hire temporaries for technical work like ours, and you can't replace these women because it's not clear that they are not returning. Most say they will return and do; but a goodly number don't, often deciding at the last minute not to, or even returning and changing their mind after a few weeks. People are good about such things and help out well and above what they have to do, but management provides no possibility for rewarding them. And if they are not rewarded, in time they will come to resent having extended themselves so far. There are problems of equity too. If you reward the person who helps out, what do you do about the outstanding worker who is on maternity leave and comes back to the job, now behind the less able worker in salary?

She went on, sympathetic yet clearly troubled:

It's a very complicated issue. It's normal to have children; women should be able to be out for a while; the company wants them back because it has an investment in their training. Not only is there a problem about getting the work done, but there is a problem around planning for the future. If they would only be honest about whether they will return—but a lot of workers are afraid that if they say they will not return, they will lose their benefit; and what's more often they can't really tell whether they will return until later, because they are not sure how they will manage a baby.

In reviewing recent experience, she talked about the pattern of return among the employees in her department. One came back for one year after childbirth and then left; a second came back after her first pregnancy, as she had said she would. Then, when she became pregnant the second time, she said she would return and did not. A third said she would not return but would take the leave she was entitled to and would resign only at the end; she did precisely this. A fourth resigned without taking her leave. A fifth came back for one week after saying she would return permanently, and then left. A sixth returned for several months—until her pension was fully vested—and then left.

Thirteen others said they would return and did and are still working. Two of those who left, now, one year later, want to return. "It's a very mixed picture, as you can see," she observed wryly.

While this department director did not design an ideal package for us, she clearly would see improvement in a situation in which employees who did not plan to return could be frank about it without losing benefits, so that the company might plan realistically. She would want some bonus money to reward those who cover for colleagues on leave. And she would probably like—on a selective basis—to be able to disregard the effect of the leave on seniority, so that superior workers are not penalized for staying out to have a child.

## Costs

Although all the companies we studied except one could provide us with estimates or approximations of the cost of the total benefit package (nonwage compensation including wages paid for time not worked), only one could give us an estimate of what the maternity benefit component might cost, and even that was very rough (table 5.1). It was based on determining the proportion of all absences that could be assigned to pregnancy disability and prorating its cost in relation to the total nonofficer payroll. That estimate, however, was for the direct dollar costs only and assumed that pregnancy disability was uniformly distributed among all salary grades. None could even begin to estimate the costs of the unpaid leave and its impact on work and productivity for obvious reasons. For the most part, where maternity leave involves a cash benefit that is paid as part of sickness benefit, no effort is made to disaggregate the two. One company estimated that between 15 and 25 percent of sick leave costs might go to maternity; another estimated maternity as 1.3 percent of disability costs. Both these estimates were clearly guesses. Two firms thought that in the future they would be in a better position to identify costs because the cost issue is increasingly important for all benefits, and they were trying to improve their data base generally.

Data on maternity are almost impossible to obtain: not only

**Table 5.1.** How One Company Estimates the Costs of Paid
Maternity Leaves

|  | 1978 | 1979 | 1980 |
|---|---|---|---|
| Leaves granted | 9 | 22 | 19 |
| Employees returning | 4 | 18 | 14 |
| Employees terminating at end of leave | 5 | 4 | 5 |
| Average number of days paid sick leave | 39 | 31 | 29 |

Absenteeism Rate

|  | Including pregnancy disabilities | Excluding pregnancy disabilities |
|---|---|---|
| June 1980 | 2.39 | 2.11 |
| July | 1.88 | 1.68 |
| Aug. | 1.98 | 1.87 |
| Sept. | 2.51 | 2.43 |
| Oct. | 3.49 | 3.04 |
| Nov. | 2.44 | 2.13 |
| Dec. | 3.08 | 2.69 |
| Jan. 1981 | 3.94 | 3.43 |
| Feb. | 3.23 | 2.92 |
| March | 2.81 | 2.30 |
| April | 2.51 | 2.18 |
| May | 2.77 | 2.26 |
| Averages | 2.75 | 2.42 |

NOTE: Pregnancy disability adds .33 days average to number of days away. Annual nonofficer payroll as of 8/78 was $8,506,886; $8,506,886 × .33 = $28,072. est. cost.

the costs of the benefit but the number of women taking leaves and the number taking personal leaves over and above the disability leaves. Employers are caught between fear of accusations of discrimination and the desire to understand better where the cost pressures are coming from.

## CHANGING ATTITUDES: IMPROVING BENEFITS

We began this book with the reminiscences of a woman who had begun to work at the end of the 1930s and had experienced a minor revolution in the policies affecting women. In summarizing the present situation concerning maternity, a much younger vice president who worked all her adult life, through her marriage and the birth and early years of her two children, commented from the perspective of the twelve years of her experience:

Maternity policies are far better than they were when I first began working. I doubt, however, that they will improve very much more. Oh, maybe women could take off another month or two—five or six months at most—but an employer can't really save a job longer than that without major dislocation. Most women employees are only having two children and most are returning to work after each birth. Coming back earlier than that is probably not good for the mother or the child. The problem for most women who want to return then is the absence of decent, affordable child care. That's the major reason some employees don't come back. In fact, I am convinced that most of the employees who plan to return do so and then quit because they just get overwhelmed because of the problems of child care.

We conclude this chapter with the comments of a personnel manager in response to our question about whether federal policies, as now designed, act as a barrier or obstacle to hiring women.

Legislation is essential, but regardless of legislation, some employers are always going to be hostile to employing women. Over my own lifetime and the years that I have been working, there has been an enormous change in attitudes and work policies. There were times in the early years when employers automatically assumed that if a woman applied for a job, she shouldn't be hired because (a) she was going to get married and quit; (b) she was going to get pregnant and quit; (c) her husband would be relocated and she would therefore go along with him and quit; (d) she would have trouble either when she was menstruating or when she was menopausal. This kind of attitude has been substantially eliminated. However, there are still old time male employers who do bring something of this towards recruitment. But the only real way change will occur is from the younger employees who are now coming into work with different kinds of attitudes and different kinds of expectations. It may be government legislation which did the prodding, but it will take time for these changes to really be integrated.

# 6. MATERNITY POLICIES: TRENDS AND ISSUES

In 1981, the following item appeared in the *Wall Street Journal:*

Ottawa, August 17: An employee benefit estimated to cost less than $1 million (Canadian) in its first year, or about 2% of the added annual cost of a new collective agreement covering Canada's postal clerks, has captured attention north of the border, winning cheers from the labor movement and drawing groans from employers' groups.

The benefit, 17 weeks of paid maternity leave at 93% of standard pay, is seen as an important precedent in a contract that last week ended a 42-day strike and closedown of Canada's postal system. . . .

[A statutory maternity benefit now provides for a 17-week job protected leave with 15 weeks covered by a special unemployment insurance benefit equal to about 60 percent of the covered wage under social insurance.]

Moreover, it's expected that the benefit will soon be negotiated in pacts covering the rest of the 300,000 unionized employees of the Canadian federal government.

Labor groups are delighted. "I hope it spreads like wildfire," says Mary Eady, head of the Women's Bureau of the Canadian Labor Congress, the nation's largest labor federation. The postal contract is a breakthrough, Miss Eady says. While similarly generous provisions were won recently in contracts covering most of Quebec province's civil servants, "the problem was to get it outside Quebec," she notes.

As it turned out, the solution was the Canadian Union of Postal Workers, a notably militant bargaining unit with about 23,000 members, 10,000 of them women. Under the union's pressures, strikes in Canada's postal system have become routine, if politically unpopular. In the latest round of bargaining, an astute union leadership let it be known that paid maternity leave was a top item on the union laundry list and that a contract wouldn't be approved without it.

Literally up against motherhood, the Canadian government gave in with regret. Donald Johnston, president of the Treasury Board and the minister responsible for government labor contracts, publicly questioned the concession. Mr. Johnston said he'd rather have put provisions for maternity pay in a legislative program than have agreed to it at the bargaining table. He didn't say whether a law is planned.

The United States is not about to enact statutory maternity benefits at the federal level. Nor have major unions made it a bargaining priority. Nor have any of the national women's organizations listed it as a high priority issue.

In a 1977 survey carried out with scientific precision, almost half the women workers who responded rated maternity leaves with pay as the least important among eighteen possible benefits.[1] No other single benefit was rated that low. In contrast, in a 1981 survey paid maternity leaves were among those benefits rated most highly and most women interviewed stated that high on their priority list was the right to a longer leave with pay.[2] Was the second sample (voluntary responses from self-selected magazine readers) too skewed to be useful? Have opinions changed so much in the brief period between the two surveys?

It is not difficult to argue that in broader societal perspective paid maternity leaves are not as important as many other benefits: for example, health insurance, pensions, and life insurance protect against many major risks that, if uncovered, could have devastating consequences for families. In another type of accounting, it could be said that certain types of health-related benefits, such as dental and vision care, may significantly benefit an entire family for an extended period, while maternity coverage is of value only for a short time, usually one or two or at most a few occasions. Even vacations occur every year and affect all family members.

Obviously, maternity leaves do not have this kind of repeated and pervasive impact. Many of those in the work force have already completed their childbearing and no longer view a maternity leave as having high priority. Young, single workers or newlyweds have often not thought far enough ahead to understand the significance of such benefits. In effect, these benefits are important to those who are pregnant or thinking about having a child, a very small group at any one point in time although a large proportion of young women workers over time. Even many of them do not always recognize or understand the potential value of such a benefit.

Moreover, this importance has only become evident in recent years. As recently as the mid-1960s most women stopped work when they became pregnant. Only 31 percent of the women giving birth in 1963 worked while pregnant, while ten years later the proportion working was 42 percent (the same proportion as worked among the nonpregnant).[3] Although precise figures are not available today, it is estimated that about 60 percent of the women giving birth in 1982 worked while pregnant. When most women left work at the time of maternity, only to return some years later when all their children were in school, the issues were very different. Public perceptions may not yet have caught up.

In addition to the substantial overall increase in female labor force participation that occurred in the 1970s, another trend emerged: more permanent labor force attachment for women. Although the figures are not exactly comparable, a 1973 survey reported that 31 percent of those women giving birth between 1971 and 1972 had returned to work within one year. By 1978, 34 percent of all married women 18 to 34 were at work within one year after childbirth and in 1981 the figure was 38 percent, this time for all women 15 to 44.[4] Among women who worked while pregnant the figure is substantially higher (62 percent in 1973), although the precise figures are not yet available for recent years. Clearly the old argument of a paid maternity leave as an extra termination benefit is no longer valid.

The maternity policy dilemma is that it can be argued that many benefits are more important. For most employees, at most times, they are. Those who need the benefits at any given time need them very much, but even they give the matter attention briefly. They do not, then, constitute, the critical mass essential to affect union negotiating strategy or legislative priorities in Washington. Groups concerned with maternal and child health or women's organizations have neither assigned the subject high priority nor effectively conveyed such a viewpoint to legislators or labor negotiators in many places.

It is not for us here to outline political strategies for whatever maternity benefit constituency might be created. We concentrate on another aspect of the dilemma—what strategies make sense with reference to the *content and form* of benefits in the light of what we have here noted and learned? Is it possible to provide coverage for most, if not all, women employees despite their locations in the labor force and the particular characteristics of maternity benefits?

## HEALTH INSURANCE

Health insurance coverage is generally regarded as the most important of all employee benefits. Now, as a result of antidiscrimination legislation, such coverage when available meets some or all of the costs of doctor and hospital at the time of childbirth, as well as any complications. However, it is worth reiterating that a recent national household survey revealed that only 66 percent of full-time female workers in the private sector (and 15 percent of all part-time workers) had such coverage in their own right.[5] Another earlier survey suggests that most of those who are not covered, however, may be covered as dependents.[6] Nevertheless, all this considered, a significant number of women workers, especially young, single (separated, divorced, or never married) women workers and wives of unemployed men are likely to remain without health insurance protection.[7] As we previously estimated, perhaps a fifth of all women in the childbearing years do not have coverage from some source. In addition, as we write we know that all of our coverage calculations are exaggerated because of the high unemployment rates late in 1982. Moreover, even when available, health insurance ranges from hospitalization coverage only, or, somewhat better, hospitalization and surgical coverage, to protection against major medical expenditures (for which the amount of protection varies greatly, too). Thus, the availability of health insurance does not, by any means, ensure even minimally adequate protection; this is available to a far smaller proportion of working women.

The potential negative consequences of this gap in coverage are underscored in a report of the findings of the 1973 National Survey of Family Growth:

Hospitalization of mothers for complications of pregnancy or hospitalization of their infants during the first year of life is more likely among women who work during the last few months of their pregnancy than among women who stop working earlier. . . . However, among women who are provided prenatal care by a private physician and among women who have insurance that pays for all or part of the hospital bill, working in the last trimester is not associated with higher rates of hospitalization. . . . Although hospitalization is but one limited indicator of pregnancy-related morbidity, it is a significant one for health economics. The reason is that the high cost of hospitalization and the high incidence of pregnancy combine to make hospitalization for pregnancy-related morbidity a significant contribution to the nation's health care costs.[8]

One could argue that assurance of basic health and medical care at the time of pregnancy and childbirth, for mothers and for their children, is the most essential element of any maternity policy.

## LEAVE

Almost all working women are entitled to a job-protected, if unpaid, leave at the time of maternity. This is a major and important accomplishment of the 1970s. Yet not all women employees have this benefit, and even for those who do the question of exactly what is meant by this guarantee still remains. Three areas of confusion about the maternity leave remain: (1) can companies maintain a policy concerning a maternity leave and still not be accused of discrimination? (2) what is meant by a comparable job on return from leave? (3) what can be done when a leave policy is announced, yet a contradictory message is conveyed by management to those making use of the leave?

In speaking to company personnel we were struck by the inconsistency with which the issue of maternity leaves is addressed. Several insisted that to maintain a nondiscriminatory policy, personal leaves for child care or "adjustment" to parenthood had to be the same for men and women, and, therefore, should be limited to a maximum of three or four months; otherwise demands for other leaves would become prohibitive. Others were quite comfortable with explicitly labeled maternity leaves, which tended to be of somewhat longer duration than other types of personal leave.

Although the concept of a gender-free policy is attractive it should not be accepted as an excuse for perpetuation of contradictions and inconsistencies in the interpretations of EEOC guidelines. This is one other indication of the primitive nature of maternity policies in the United States even now. There are many legal, administrative, and legislative roads to clarity, all of which could be explored, but few have been tried.

Many legal experts today are convinced that while establishing a special maternity leave would be against the law, a special parental or child care leave is not. Thus, a gender-free policy can be maintained providing special protection for a newborn and for the parent-child relationship. Such a policy would enable employers to permit a somewhat longer post-childbirth leave, even if unpaid, for those who want a little more time and can manage it economically. Most of the takers would probably be women—as seen even in Sweden, which has the most liberal of policies.

Similarly, efforts are needed to achieve clarity on the definition of a comparable job; questions about this are still emerging in complaints and legal actions. Both administrative rulings and legal decisions will gradually specify the concept.

The "mixed signal" problem is more complex. Cultural change and legal action should gradually make it possible for a parent to exercise the right to a leave without facing career penalties. However, the process can be slow, particularly in the midst of a slack labor market.

A major issue that is addressed most inconsistently is the extent to which women on some form of unpaid maternity leave continue to be covered by other employee benefits (e.g., health insurance) and whether these are to be paid by employers (if they are so paid when the employee is at work), or if the employee now becomes routinely liable for their costs once on leave. Perhaps all of this is a question for individual and collective bargaining related to the conditions of employment. On the other hand, legal issues may be raised. Clarity and dissemination of information would be in order.

## HOW MANY HAVE INCOME PROTECTION AND HOW MANY DO NOT?

Despite the growing acceptance of unpaid but protected maternity leaves, the issue of income protection remains, at the beginning of the 1980s, a continuing concern. This is a major issue, perhaps *the* major issue. The 1978 Pregnancy Discrimination Act is assumed by many in industry and in some business associations to have led to almost complete coverage of women employees, ensuring the replacement of at least some portion of their lost wages for some period of time around childbirth, "usually up to eight weeks." Our review of the current situation suggests that coverage is much less extensive than popularly believed. Indeed, the estimates of coverage in 1977, used at the time of the hearings on the Discrimination Act, were probably unrealistically high to begin with. Here we must elaborate and sum up.

If we include the states having temporary disability insurance (TDI), since these plans now offer benefits for pregnancy and maternity, about half the nongovernmental or private-sector workers, at most, are covered by some form of disability or sickness insurance benefits, providing income replacement for about six to eight weeks at the time of a normal childbirth (see table 4.4). Excluding responses from these five states, less than half the employers in our survey provide such benefit. Yet let us note (1) bias in our sample (and, therefore, these estimates) toward medium and large firms, or toward smaller firms with high net worth; and (2) the heavy concentration of women employees in small establishments with low net worth. In light of these considerations a more accurate coverage figure would probably be less than 40 percent of working women. By the standards of major industrial societies and in relation to a broader concept of what is needed, however, this is hardly an admirable picture. Even in the most generous situations, no firm and no state provides for a paid maternity leave that lasts more than an *absolute maximum* of twelve weeks and most provide far less or none at all; no country in Europe, even the least generous, provides less than fourteen weeks, and most provide far more.

Furthermore, the issue of equity is ever present. For most working women, whether or not they have any kind of job and income protection at the time of childbirth is a function of where they live, where they work, whether or not they are married, and where their husbands work. Surely, this suggests that something is awry in our country.

Having offered our best estimate, however, we would stress the problems in obtaining reliable coverage data. The existing employer surveys are not based on representative samples of employers. All are either biased toward large and medium firms or involved self-selected or purposive rather than random samples. Our own mail survey was constrained by available sampling frames. The major gaps in information are for small employers. Household surveys have only begun to obtain data on employee benefits from the employee perspective. Only pensions and health insurance have been looked at thus far.[9] The QES, the only national survey of employees, has not been repeated since 1977. All existing data sources on benefits other than pensions, health insurance, and possibly, life insurance, have sampling biases that would seem to overstate coverage.

While our estimates are only that, a report published after our own calculations were completed suggests that we are approximately accurate. A Social Security Administration study, "Cash Benefits for Short-Term Sickness, 1979," deals with private sector coverage for sickness by a short-term disability plan, sick pay insurance, or a sick leave plan—and in states with or without state TDI plans. According to this study,[10] about 63 percent of *all* wage and salary workers, including 89 percent of government employees, 57 percent of wage and salary workers in the private sector in all states with TDI, and 44 percent of private sector workers in states without TDI, were covered by one of these three networks. If we exclude from our estimate brief sick leave plan coverage as being inadequate for any real income protection at the time of maternity, our estimates (table 4.4) are compatible with those in this report.

Regardless, even by the most generous estimate, at least half of the private female labor force does *not* have income and job protection at the time of childbirth. Unlike health insurance protection, which may be available as a dependent's entitlement, a maternity benefit can be earned only in one's own right.

Admittedly, the summing up is not quite complete since some additional employees may draw upon paid sick leave and vacation time in connection with pregnancy and childbirth. We in fact found that they do.

Nobody would deny that such coverage for the income protection aspect of maternity is better than nothing. However, it changes our numbers very little and it clearly does not begin to be enough. For one thing, the companies with temporary disability and long-term disability coverage have the more generous vacation policies. More important, vacation policy in the United States is generally very limited, so that entitlements are brief and accrual very slow. The women in the least attractive jobs and young women who have worked only a few years will not be able to "package" much paid time off when they give birth. As a consequence, even for those with such protection only about four weeks at most would be covered for maternity purposes, which is not enough. Moreover, such use of vacation or sick time would leave the employee with no vacation and no margin for getting sick, both additional stresses at an already stressful period in the woman's—and her child and family's— life cycle. The self-employed, domestics, and women in unskilled service jobs are at a particular disadvantage here; they are likely to have no entitlement.

In short, sick leave and vacation policies are not a solution to income protection at the time of childbirth.

## THE MORE FORTUNATE HALF?

We need to look further at what is actually available for the 40 (or even 50) percent with the "more adequate" coverage. In the context of concern about sex discrimination, employed women have earned some basic protection for themselves during pregnancy and at the time of and immediately following childbirth. The device used to protect the earnings of women workers as well as their jobs is entitlement to sickness or short-term disability benefits, on the premise that pregnancy and maternity are disabling conditions. Thus, women experiencing such condition should qualify for the same benefits provided for any other disability. In other words, for social policy purposes, pregnancy and maternity are defined as disabilities. If job and income protection exist for any disability, maternity is covered in the same way; if such protection does not exist, employers are under no obligation to provide the benefit.

Typically, what such benefits bring is partial (or, occasionally, full) replacement of earnings while the employee is defined as disabled. In the case of normal delivery, this usually means a benefit duration of about six weeks after childbirth (and sometimes one or two weeks before). Although there are variations in the length of time a worker may stay home before giving birth, usually reflecting the physical demands of different types of work, as locally interpreted, the post-childbirth leave has emerged as a much more uniform benefit. A period of six to eight weeks after birth has become the standard benefit for a normal delivery under both statutory TDI and private plans, though it varies from four to ten weeks, overall. Despite some concern at the time of the 1977 hearings and following passage of the 1978 legislation, employers and their insurance companies have developed a fairly consistent pattern regarding this period of disability.

The medical basis for defining this standard seems to derive from a medical view of women during the post-childbirth period as being physiologically vulnerable. This six- to eight-week period after childbirth is termed the puerperium and viewed as a time of special vulnerability to disease. According to one recognized authority, writing in a standard text on obstetrics and gynecology: "The puerperium is that variable period, usually 6–8 weeks beginning with the delivery of the placenta and ending with the resumption of ovulatory menstrual cycles in an otherwise normal woman. . . . This is the time when there are not only continued but new risks of disease." [11] Complicated deliveries are usually covered, however, for a longer period, often under long-term disability benefits. Yet the physiologically based definitions of disability have not won full acceptance among all employers, as some pressure their workers for a quicker return to work.

While the benefit duration is fairly consistent, the variation in the benefit levels is significant. State TDI benefits are uniformly low and usually similar to unemployment insurance benefits. Most private plans replace about 60 to 70 percent of earnings, and long-term plans provide a higher wage replacement rate than short-term benefits. Needless to say, women professionals and executives are assured far greater income protection than women in blue-, pink-, or even many routine white-collar jobs.

Since these are tax-free benefits, the net loss in disposable income to the employee can be negligible in the most generous plans. Moreover, in many large and medium-sized firms in states providing TDI, the employer helps employees to package the two so as to come as close as possible to a full wage. Such packaging may involve the use of a paid sick leave (current and accrued), paid vacation time, short- or long-term disability payments, and state TDI benefits.

Of particular importance, of course, is that income protection varies enormously, especially for "average" workers. They have very little if they depend on a packaging of sickness and vacation pay alone, do far better with private temporary disability benefits, and may come close to full protection if they have supplementary temporary or long-term disability benefits in a company plan in a state with statutory TDI.

For low-wage earning women, women in agricultural jobs, and women working for small employers or in the retail service sector, the location of their jobs in states with or without statutory TDI is the major factor determining whether or not they are protected at all. Working in different geographic locations, even though for the same employer, can lead to serious inequities in the kinds of benefits employees receive.

## JOB PROTECTION

Although half the labor force may qualify for a paid maternity leave with "full" job protection, discriminatory policies have still not ended, even for these employees. The issue may no longer be whether they are entitled to benefits and whether their job is to be held for them. Instead, the issues of sex discrimination have been refocused on the question of how long a woman is disabled and how long she is entitled to receive a disability benefit. Some employers pressure women to return to work sooner, threatening loss of benefits or jobs if they do not. Others, for a variety of reasons, find it impossible to return a women to her previous job, and the argument is over job comparability. For still others the problem emerges in initial hiring. Some employers continue to be leery of engaging young married women, on the assumption that they may become pregnant and have to be "carried" as nonproductive workers for two months. Finally, as suggested earlier, some other employers announce a policy, but communicate a message to their female employees suggesting that an extended leave, even if technically permitted, would lead to an assessment of the worker as "less than fully committed" to her work. This is especially so for professionals and executives.

Sex discrimination thus remains and is played out indirectly, if not directly, as women become pregnant and rear children. It seems likely that as long as women are viewed as carrying primary responsibility for child rearing (in addition to their full responsibility for childbearing), discrimination will remain. As long as policies related to parenting continue to be labeled maternity questions, the situation will only be exacerbated.

## PREGNANCY AND MATERNITY AS DISABILITY

It is difficult to overstate the consequences of defining pregnancy and maternity as a disability "like any other illness," as one is told countless times in company after company. Viewing maternity as an illness means that it is the woman alone who is the target of the policy. As soon as she is physically capable of returning to work, she should do so. U.S. employment practices with regard to pregnancy and childbirth seem to reflect the most niggardly approach of any advanced industrialized country, and defining maternity as a disability seems only to reinforce this. The International Labor Organization (ILO) Conventions of 1952, never signed by the United States even though almost all other member countries have signed it, sets fourteen weeks as the standard, six before birth and eight after. Many of the countries that have not extended that minimum, now, at least, permit the fourteen weeks to be taken either before or after birth as long as at least six weeks are taken after. The increasingly prevalent medical view is that women can work until, or close to, the end of pregnancy, depending on the type of work as well as personal health, and most women want a longer post-childbirth leave. In contrast, the U.S. practice seems to be that if a woman can work until the end of her pregnancy that is fine, but her post-childbirth leave is still to be limited to the period that she is physically disabled.

There is something perhaps even more fundamental. The major difference between U.S. and European practice is not just the presence or absence of a statutory social insurance benefit but differences in ideology and philosophy concerning maternity and the childbearing function. Whereas maternity benefits and leaves were initially defined in Europe as a form of health protection for the mother, this is no longer the case. In the course of the 1970s, maternity policies have gone well beyond this narrow focus on maternal health protection to encompass the much broader role of providing support for mother-child or parent-child relationships, child care, and, most important, child development. It is in this context that many countries extended their paid maternity leaves very significantly during the last decade (and extended their unpaid but fully job-protected supplementary leaves still further).

The child development component of maternity policy is seldom dealt with at all today in the United States, either in the policy debate or in the discussion of benefits and related employer practices. There are occasional exceptions. At the time of the 1977 hearings one participant commented (in criticism) that a mother's decision to take time off after childbirth could be inspired not by her own disability but by her desire to take care of her infant: "No disability plan makes provision for the employee to receive benefits to serve the natural needs of another family member." Moreover, the argument continues, if we were to establish a benefit that permits or encourages this we will be creating a problem of great inequity in the employee benefit systems.

Our own view is that the parenting and child development components of a maternity leave constitute a significant aspect of the policy that has received nowhere near the attention it warrants. So far the concern has been primarily with protecting women against job loss and the loss of other existing, related entitlements. Job protection and health insurance protection have been primary, supplemented by concern for a modest amount of income protection for a brief period of time. These are worthy objectives and we have outlined areas for improvement. That disability insurance represented a readily available device for providing a benefit seems clear. It is less clear whether the choice of the disability route ever embodied any real concern for parent-child relationships. Or, if there was concern, whether it was displaced onto the argument of those who opposed mothers' employment altogether. Regardless, current national policy has slighted maternity as a condition leading to parenthood and overlooked the welfare of the baby as well.

Using disability insurance as a device for protecting against income loss at the time of maternity may be understandable, and even reasonable, in a country with no national health insurance system. Losing track of maternity as parenthood and treating it as if it really were an illness is neither. The Canadians, after all, use unemployment insurance for the same purpose— to protect against income loss at the time of maternity. Certainly, that is at least as imperfect a device as disability insurance. However, (1) it is part of their national social insurance system, and (2) they separate the special unemployment insurance benefit providing maternity protection from the conventional types of unemployment benefit. As a consequence, job protection is mandated nationally for seventeen weeks and income protection for fifteen. There is nothing in the concept of disability that by itself precludes special attention to maternity apart from an insistence in the United States that the term disability be applied medically and literally. Otherwise, for example, states providing TDI could define the period of disability for normal pregnancies and childbirth as twelve, sixteen, or even twenty weeks, depending on the value placed on protecting the early mother-child relationship. After all, is this any more arbitrary than defining old age as 65 for the purpose of qualifying for social security old age insurance?

This seeming loss of the baby—and of parenthood—in setting our maternity policy seems especially strange in the country that leads the world in expertise in child development research. We will return to the question of how this skew or imbalance can be corrected. Until it is, the United States will not have an adequate maternity policy worthy of its economic capabilities or moral stature.

## EMPLOYERS HAVE PROBLEMS, TOO

So far we have talked only of the problems existing maternity policies present for employees. Employers have problems, too. For some the problem is one of direct benefit costs. The price of benefits to employers reflects in part the scale of their enterprise. It may not be feasible for employers who have four or five employees to purchase certain types of insurance. It will be even more difficult if they have one or two. Even if they want to do their share, small employers find it difficult to take on costs not assumed by local competition. When they must choose, they may decide that a basic benefit such as health insurance is all that is possible, if they can manage that.

Cost factors were a major concern of employers at the 1977 hearings. Even for those to whom competitive costs and profit margins are not central, however, work dislocation is a potential problem. Whether it is a small firm (e.g., a doctor's office, a coffee shop) or a large firm with multiple units, many of which are female labor intensive, the potential for work problems is readily apparent.

We do not wish to overstate the issue. For many firms, there may not be any work dislocation or coverage problem. In many medium-sized units, no worker, or only one or two, is on maternity leave at any one time. This was the case in two-thirds of the firms in our survey. At large organizations more employees are apt to be on maternity leave, but they are also likely to be in different units and the contribution of any one or even a few employees is not likely to be crucial to the functioning of the company. However, at small work sites even one worker's absence can be a problem if she is a skilled or specialized worker. It can be a major problem if she is out for four or five months. Certainly two or more out at the same time can create a crisis in a small unit. There are potential coverage and work-dislocation problems in a significant number of places and that, too, cannot be ignored.

The historical solution was not to hire women or to replace them permanently when they become pregnant. There are workable alternatives, but until they are adopted adequate maternity policy will be found only in large companies or units with the kind of work readily picked up by temporaries, a good number of people who do the same work, or ability to make provision for a co-worker to learn the absent woman's tasks so as to provide coverage during leave.

These conditions are met in many places and we do not minimize them. For the others, solutions will require adoption of

— devices whereby small employers may purchase certain coverage together, to achieve some of the economy of scale available to larger employers;
— policies that permit women who do not intend to return after childbirth to report this early, to ensure adequate replacement, yet not suffer adverse benefit consequences;
— more extensive use of part-time, half-time, and phased-in return to work after childbirth;
— efforts to increase the scope and size of the pool of part-time personnel who provide coverage.

One further comment on the plight of the small firm may be in order. We note that European countries with statutory benefit and leave policies do apply them uniformly. Once they are universal, such practices do not create competitive advantages and disadvantages. The nonstatutory pattern in the United States makes it particularly difficult for the small employer to be generous and not to suffer disadvantage.

It is said that the possible inconvenience or even serious dislocations in the work place that follow from any but the briefest of leaves explains the continuing, if hard-to-prove, hiring discrimination that affects young women of childbearing age, especially where the labor market is slack. This we assume will continue to some extent until solutions of the sort described above are implemented and found to be adequate. It would be controlled, however, by other statutory or administrative policies that converted maternity benefits in the post-childbirth period into parental benefits. If a significant number of young fathers took leaves (or at least had the legal right to take leaves), women would not be defined as especially large risks. This of course is a policy for a time when the leave allows more than time for physical recovery from disability and includes additional time for parenting. If presented with the possibility of part-time jobs with adequate benefits and career potential, some parents might even opt for each working part time. Each could work three days a week, for example, between them managing complete care of their own baby at a time when at-home child care is difficult to come by and expensive.

## A PUBLIC-PRIVATE MIX

We began this exploration as part of a broader interest in how employers were responding to certain obvious changes in the labor force, and with what consequences. The maternity benefit and leave issues seemed to be relatively defined, manageable, and significant.

By now we know that it is not a simple story. Data are difficult to assemble, particularly for the small firms where large proportions of women workers are employed. Coverage of doctor and hospital costs is reported reasonably well. Other things are reported for middle-sized and larger companies. But we discovered that even what is defined as generous and adequate in such companies is often limited. There are problems about job protection if leaves are "too long," and income protection is available to fewer workers and for far less than the available leave time.

One discrepancy derives from a definition of the issue and from past legal strategies to ensure women's rights, probably in the reverse order. The labor market is not yet ready to attract and retain female workers by reaching out to meet all their family needs. The U.S. labor market, after all, has not been that tight, because female labor force participation exploded in the 1960 to 1980 era and the supply was large. On the other hand, the decade of the 1970s was one of major progress in women's rights. Those who fought to end discrimination therefore were able to seize upon health insurance, sickness benefits, and temporary disability insurance and to make them resources for pregnant women.

In those instances where companies had developed generous maternity leave and pay policies, and there were some, the new laws were sometimes interpreted as constraints. Such companies decided that special considerations connected with maternity would be defined as discriminating against men and would open the way to costly add-ons. A few companies therefore cut back, not on paid leaves, but on the length of the unpaid, job-protected leaves they provided.

For the overwhelming majority of women workers, however, the antidiscrimination approach was progress. As we have seen, the legislation stated that if a company awards temporary disability benefits to anybody for any purpose, whether as a result of a union contract or its own initiatives, it cannot then exclude pregnancy and childbirth as causing disabilities. This legislation has become the most important basis for ensuring income protection during maternity leaves. It apparently was the source of considerable improvement in the situations of many working women.

Yet the very nature of the reform defined its advantages and limitations. It is a social policy "Catch 22." The leave before childbirth is determined by the physical demands of the work, as interpreted by the doctor. Much unnecessary insistence that women remain at home because they are pregnant has ended.

But the leave after childbirth is also medically determined, according to physical "recovery." Convention has by now settled on six or eight weeks, and there are some medical rationales. The fact that it is never *seven* weeks makes one wonder.

In any case, "good" plans now involve eight weeks of disability. Sometimes paid vacation or sick leave is added. This is an improvement, but the post-childbirth leave duration is less than that in most advanced industrial countries. Unpaid leave may be added, but most women cannot afford that, and many companies constrict such leave for all employees. If one is not back soon, the job could be gone. Few permit more than four months in toto, including both paid and unpaid leave. In effect, the duration of unpaid but job-protected leaves is thus also far less than what is prevalent in European countries.

Unexpectedly, we discovered that the situation was best for women who need maternity leaves in the five states with statutory temporary disability requirements. "Unexpectedly" because we knew that wage replacement was limited and duration "short." But in those states, all women do have the six or eight weeks (and sometimes more) of income protection. If they work in enlightened companies, the state benefit is integrated with the company benefit and there is either a longer leave or a higher wage replacement, or both.

Inevitably, the typical practice becomes the standard and the norm, yet we have noted that this is a trap. Six or eight weeks of paid maternity leave is not enough for parents or for children in one of the richest countries in the world, a country that has developed basic knowledge about child development and parenting. Many parents want and could use some more time to develop their new roles and relationships. In such instances it is highly likely that children would benefit.

The policy challenges, then, are twofold:

— to attempt to ensure that all women have no less protection than what can be offered by state temporary disability plans;
— to find some way to add parenting time to what is now a physical disability leave.

As a practical matter, this is a two-stage process. However, given the geographic and industry diversity in the United States,

each can be pursued differently, by different groups, responding to different constitutencies.

## WHERE WILL CHANGE COME FROM?

### Women's Organizations and The Women's Movement

Although the women's movement clearly has played an important role in improving the status of women, maternity and
other family benefits have not been at the forefront of its agenda.
Indeed, not even the inadequacy of child care services—an issue
working mothers have identified as the single most important
problem they face in coping with work and family life—was
high on the agenda of the women's movement until very recently. In some respects their broad goals have been more am-
bitious: an end to discrimination, achievement of equal rights
and equal pay, and the end of occupational segregation. Their
short-range targets have been more immediate, including particular attention to abortion rights and passage of the Equal
Rights Amendment to the Constitution.

Betty Friedan has urged the women's movement to develop
a family-oriented perspective and support a family policy agenda.
The response to her call has been mixed. Heretofore, the wom-
en's movement has viewed family policies either as too tradi-
tional a focus for enlightened women, or as too open to criticism as conservative. With family issues becoming increasingly
politicized women's organizations along a broad political spec-
trum have begun to realize that a more assertive stance on family issues is essential if those issues central to women are not to
be taken over by others less sensitive to the needs, wants, and
preferences of the majority of women. Given the centrality of
the family relationship in women's lives, it seems hard to argue
that such issues should not be high on the policy agenda.

Although its advocates have not yet achieved the critical mass
of which we have spoken, we hope that the great importance of
the maternity-parenting issue will gain increasing visibility and
support. Recently, such organizations as the National Organization for Women (NOW) have finally begun to take a strong
position in support of policies such as these. Clearly, if women's

organizations fail to take a strong and visible position on the importance of maternity leaves and benefits, it is hard to argue that any other sector should take the initiative. Self-interest, if nothing else, should propel women in this direction.

## Organized Labor

As is well documented, benefits in general tend to be more extensive in unionized companies than nonunionized companies, though to date unionized firms have not taken a leading role in pressing for maternity benefits. Some of those companies that are unionized or partially unionized do view the unions as becoming increasingly concerned about such benefits. At the same time others claim that management introduced disability benefits covering maternity without any encouragement from organized labor. Indeed, the management of some particularly generous firms, whose benefit plans have been shaped by union pressures, have commented on the absence of attention even from unions heavily dominated by female members.

Organized labor has not made these benefits a major cause despite the interests of a few female-intensive units and despite the growing numbers of their male members who have working wives. We expect the subject to gain in attention if current economic problems can in some significant way be resolved, so that collective bargaining may reexamine its benefits agenda. A benefit that increases equity for women could have appeal in some quarters; however, so far organized labor has paid little attention to women and women's issues of all types, not just maternity policies.

In contrast to the role played by organized labor in the United States, unions have played an important role in other countries in taking the initiative in supporting women's and family-related policies. Parent insurance, maternity benefits, and child care services have all been priorities of the trade union organizations of countries such as France and Sweden. The most recent Canadian development (higher maternity benefit levels) occurred as a consequence of actions taken by a Canadian union. Although organized labor is far less important in the United States than in Europe (23 percent of the U.S. labor force are union members as compared with 50 percent in France and Germany and 70 percent in Sweden), it still has a significant potential for influencing the development of those policies it chooses to support. Moreover, if organized labor hopes to expand its membership, working women represent a major unrepresented constituency: less than 15 percent of working women are union members. If labor does not take a strong position in support of this and other policies of importance to women it is hard to see why women would choose to identify with unions today. Certainly, if labor wants to expand its role in white-collar jobs and the service industries, it is going to have to pay more attention to these issues.

## Management

We have been told by management personnel in several large manufacturing companies that companies in industries in which labor costs are a relatively small proportion of total cost can be generous with benefit provisions. It is good for morale, good publicity, and inexpensive. Industry competitiveness is stressed as an important factor. Once the "leading edge" firms establish a policy or give a benefit all others will follow, more or less rapidly.

Labor scarcity and the desire to recruit and retain labor, especially highly skilled labor, was a factor listed repeatedly for nonunionized high technology firms even during the 1982 recession. Ultimately, this may be most important, yet progress cannot wait until there are labor shortages everywhere.

It is not clear whether and how much of American industry will initiate something more like the emerging pattern in Europe, five or six months of paid leave, with a job guarantee, for those women who want to take advantage of it. Such leave provides for replacement of the full salary, or salary minus social security deductions. There is provision as well for benefit continuance, and there is provision for supplementary leaves, usually for up to one year, that are unpaid but ensure full job protection, seniority, and pension entitlements.

Certainly more firms could do this than now do, especially if state TDI provisions extend nationwide. Leading companies will find it an attractive and not overly expensive way to retain personnel or to recruit. This will occur only where the economic situation of the company is good and where recruitment and retention, as essential for effective competition, are recognized aims. The number of such companies is likely to increase as the economy recovers from the 1982 recession.

An extended paid leave may not be everywhere feasible, even for well-situated companies, because of work disruption and job coverage problems. Some women may not want to be out of work quite that long because of their commitments to their jobs and their career advancement goals. Under such circumstances private employers could add a parenting component that would not be too costly by establishing in their companies a right to part-time jobs (three-day weeks or six-hour days) for those with children under 1 year of age. There is some successful experience with such efforts already. It would identify a company as in the lead and eager to attract and hold qualified women who also want to be parents. Such a right would permit parents a transitional period, following the birth of a new baby. With benefits protected and the right to part-time work available to both men and women with very young children, the likelihood of women carrying the full burden of maternity and parenting—and a concomitant penalty at work—would be attenuated. It would help two-earner and two-career families move closer toward parenting equity.

## The Role of Government

Ultimately, as we examine the history of the 1970s, the role of court cases, EEOC regulations, pension legislation, and the 1978 Pregnancy Disability Amendments, one is reminded again that government must be part of such forward thrusts. Public policy creates rights and benefits, but it does more. It defines norms, sets standards, and defines community expectations.

One question raised repeatedly is why have extensive maternity benefits been legislated throughout Europe and the industrialized world generally, yet not gained any support in the United States. Obviously, here we are speculating; we have carried out systematic analyses elsewhere on the factors accounting for differences in child policies without reaching any definite conclusions.[12] Regardless, we suggest the following as possible factors.

Some form of national health insurance exists in almost all industrialized countries. Not only does such a benefit assure pregnant women of good, free prenatal and postnatal care, pediatric care for new infants, and hospital and physician care, but it provides a readily available system for highlighting the significance of maternity as a life cycle stage and improving the protection of women and children at this important time. For those concerned especially with maternal and child health, the relationship between a national health policy and maternity policy seems very close. Although about sixteen countries have managed to develop maternity policies while not having a national health insurance program, it is undoubtedly easier to do so when such a program is in place.

Second, concern with the well-being of children is a far more visible and deliberate policy target in many other countries than it is in the United States. Child benefits—child or family allowances, for example—are a standard policy throughout the world, but not in the United States. A view of governmental activity as appropriate, indeed desirable, where the well-being of children is concerned, leads to a widespread expectation regarding society's obligation to children that goes beyond mere rhetoric. Although concern with a declining birth rate is far more prevalent in several European countries than here, there are many countries without such concern where attention to children nonetheless remains high on the public agenda. Americans, by contrast, have hesitated about apparent governmental involvement in explicit family policy.

Female labor force participation rates alone are a necessary but insufficient factor contributing to the development of maternity policies for working women. Yet countries with far lower proportions of women at work than in the United States have instituted such policies. On the other hand, given the current political scene, as mentioned earlier, the active and strong support of organized labor in countries in which organized labor plays an important role in national policy making has made a difference.

The United States is unlikely, in the immediate future, to establish either a national health insurance program or any kind of a national child or family policy. Concern with the limitations of "big government" far outweighs the potential benefits, at least for now. It seems clear that a national statutory maternity policy is unlikely to be legislated in the near future. This, however, does not mean there can be no role for government.

Indeed, in pointing out the significance of the federal government's role in the development of whatever policy has emerged, one very forthright human resource officer stated:

Where maternity is concerned, really one thing made the difference: government legislation and regulations. Sure we began to think about changing our policies as we hired more women but we only began to do anything when the EEOC guidelines were issued. That real push came after passage of the Pregnancy Act. That, combined with the government's affirmative action regulations was what really got us moving. Once we changed our policies and established a new maternity benefit we all agreed it made great sense. By then we had many more women on board, and it seemed like good labor relations policy. But we'd have been much slower if it weren't for the government. It's too unimportant a benefit where most workers are concerned and too different and new an initiative where management is concerned.

Another offered a supplementary perspective.

What may make a difference in the future are the changes that are occurring in the personal lives and families of top management, and in the composition of middle level management staff now on their way up. More of our top executives have wives—maybe second wives, it's true, who are career women; and they have daughters and daughters-in-law who are professionals and managers themselves. You can't help but have your views and values affected by hearing your own family members talk. And as more women come up the management ladder they're giving us a different view of benefits—and other employment practices. They are bound to have an effect.

Community norms, government rules, and management enlightenment out of personal and family experience—all can be important forces.

# ACHIEVING THE MINIMUM

Those who are eager to ensure most women at least a minimum of coverage might explore the possibility of state TDI legislation in the forty-five states without it.

Despite the limitations and inadequacies of state TDI benefits, they do provide an enormously important foundation or "safety net," depending on one's perspective. The state of the economy and national politics as we write could make that a more productive avenue than a search for a national TDI statute. State regulations and their variants create an annoyance for national and regional companies, but they are the price of current preferences for devolution.

Our explorations in the states with such legislation have not been of sufficient depth to explain why five states provide statutory benefits and others have not. Although all who do are heavily metropolitan and highly populous, there are others with similar characteristics that do not offer such provisions.

State plans are inexpensive and do not constitute a financial burden on employers or employees. The existing state funds are all in excellent shape. The California plan, in fact, had a large surplus; it reduced its tax rate substantially and provided a rebate to participants.

A state TDI as a guarantor of a maternity benefit safety net solves a number of additional problems already mentioned. Among the small businesses, since it is compulsory and has uniform cost, it avoids giving a competitive advantage to the employer who, in a voluntary system, refuses to respond to employee needs over the one who does. It also provides a vehicle for coverage of women who work but happen to be unemployed at the time of childbirth.

A state plan is the most promising coverage vehicle, as well, for the self-employed and domestic servants. Variations in benefit level and coverage may remain and inequities continue, but at the very least, if available in all states such a policy would reduce current inequities significantly.

State action need not interfere with the kind of initiatives currently taken by companies on their own or as a result of collective bargaining. On the contrary, state TDI benefits can provide a baseline that individual firms can supplement in a variety of ways. Four of the states with TDI provision, but not Rhode Island, permit companies to provide their own alternatives on the basis of equivalent or superior coverage; supplementary coverage can, of course, be provided. This combination of public and private provisions is a good idea.

While acknowledging that six to eight weeks are insufficient, we have outlined an approach to achieving it for more or most female workers. It is not enough, however, if the parenting component is to have attention in the long run.

Perhaps some leadership groups in the professions (medicine, child development, pediatrics) might be willing to convene experts to address the importance of the parenting experience and the significance of a more extended period of protected time for mother and child for those wishing it, without the penalty of financial loss.

In a complementary action, perhaps some leadership groups among business executives could convene a group of their colleagues from major firms in France, Germany, and Scandinavia to explore how they manage the more extended paid leaves and how they view this type of social protection.

And perhaps also some leadership groups among women in management might convene a group of U.S. and international experts to address the significance of these benefits to women, children, and men in this and other countries and explore possible alternatives leading to the development of improved policies in the United States.

While these are our hopes, the need for such initiative will only grow. Through periods of economic growth and recession as well, more women are working outside the home and continuing to work even while pregnant and after childbirth. Those women and their husbands will continue to need and to seek a consistent and equitable maternity policy that will consider maternal health, child development, and family well-being. In responding, the society will and must reflect the needs of employers, as well.

American social policy currently favors the strengthening of public-private partnerships. In five states, a state temporary disability minimum provides a platform on which to build additional responsiveness to parenting. Forty-five states do not yet have such provision. There cannot be a partnership without a public actor. That is where the next initiative could begin.

This country protects family privacy and individual autonomy by foregoing comprehensive public policy initiatives. Unlike some countries, it does not ask broadly: "What is good for families? What should the society do?" But we do look at *specific* needs, problems, gaps. Maternity policy is integral to our core values and ideology. Even if we are not prepared to do more, at the very least this modest, limited, inexpensive policy, of such clear value for children, mothers, and fathers, warrants active support.

# Appendix. MATERNITY BENEFITS IN THE PRIVATE SECTOR: STUDY DESIGN AND METHODOLOGY

## POPULATION AND SAMPLING FRAMES

For most practical considerations, the population of our survey of corporations is incorporated businesses with a net worth of at least $500,000 in 1980. More specifically, however, the population is restricted to firms included in Dunn and Bradstreet, *Million Dollar Directory*, volumes 1 and 2. (These two volumes were used as the sampling frames for the survey.) The basic requirement for a company's inclusion in volume 1 is a net worth of at least $1,000,000; for volume 2, a net worth of $500,000 to $999,999.*

While the combined listings of volume 1 and 2 are very large (some 90,000 companies) and represent the most inclusive list available for drawing a sample, they are not fully inclusive of all companies meeting one of these criteria. Unfortunately, the characteristics of the excluded companies (with a net worth of at least $500,000) are not systematically known. By Dunn and

We have prepared this report for the general reader. Research specialists who may have additional questions about method are invited to communicate directly with the authors at their universities.
*Also eligible are domestic subsidiaries of foreign corporations and subsidiaries having less than qualifying net worth themselves but deriving comparable financial strength from a formal arrangement with the parent company.

Bradstreet's informal account, foreign corporations, professional and consulting agencies, credit agencies, and some other types of financial and insurance companies are all under-represented to some indeterminate degree. Since the characteristics of the population of firms with a net worth of at least $500,000 are unknown, the representativeness of the Dunn and Bradstreet firms in relation to this population cannot be systematically assessed. Technically, then, because there is no exhaustive (or putatively representative) listing of all American companies, the sampling frames define the population of the study. Nonetheless, broadly speaking, the Dunn and Bradstreet directories may be said to include a diverse and probably reasonably representative listing of firms with at least modest net worth. For the purposes of our rough estimates, they should be adequate.

One obvious limitation in using the Dunn and Bradstreet directories as a sampling frame deserves special emphasis: as measured by net worth, the very smallest businesses—predominantly service and trade—are excluded from the analysis. In general, most of these firms may be assumed to have relatively few employees, but it should be recognized that 26 percent of the labor force works at companies with fewer than 20 employees and about half work for firms with fewer than 100 employees. We therefore cannot report on the maternity-related policies of a significant segment of private business.

On the other hand, while this exclusion cannot be overlooked, most very small firms with fewer than twenty to twenty-five employees would seem unlikely to have formal maternity *policies*. Many of these small firms have never or only rarely had to deal with a childbearing employee. Of course their informal practices or ad hoc arrangements are important for the affected families, but is unlikely that these arrangements are even minimally accommodating in any consistent way to women at the time of birth. Survey questions about the maternity policies of these companies would therefore have very little meaning. Yet, even if a mail survey is inappropriate for analyzing how pregnant employees are treated in this segment of the economy, it should be recognized that any projections about maternity policies in the private sector are affected by this exclusion.

# THE SAMPLE AND RESPONSE

The two Dunn and Bradstreet directories were treated as one sampling frame, and 1,000 companies were systematically selected for inclusion in the sample. Companies were selected from the alphabetized lists at prespecified intervals. An initial mailing to the companies was sent in late 1980; all companies not responding to this request were sent another mailing in early 1981.

We received 200 responses; 10 of the questionnaires were not completed because the companies did not have any female employees. Excluding the 15 companies with undeliverable addresses from the sample, the response rate for usable questionnaires is about 20 percent.

We decided that the response to the mail survey was small, especially for analysis of practices in smaller firms in particular industries. We therefore augmented the responses to the mail survey with 50 telephone interviews. These telephone interviews were not as detailed as the mail survey, but they included items that largely replicated questions in the mail survey. (We note on the facsimile of the mail questionnaire, included at the end of this appendix, which items were included in the telephone survey.)

Companies in the telephone survey were selected from the original sample of 1,000 on a purposive basis. Since we had relatively few responses from trade and service establishments, and smaller firms generally, these kinds of companies were selected for focused attention. Telephone interviews were conducted with companies in these industrial categories: service, wholesale trade, retail trade, and small manufacturing. Within each category, companies were systematically selected.

Thus, in effect, we stratified the original sample by industrial classifications and drew small systematic samples within selected strata. We set a quota of 50 completed interviews. Only a few firms could not be reached, and in these cases we randomly substituted other firms within the same sampling stratum. There were no refusals of telephone interviews by firms which we located.

The survey is thus primarily based on a systematic (non-technically, random) sample of companies of at least modest worth which has been augmented by a small, systematic sample of selected strata of the original sample. The reason for pursuing this strategy was to augment the response from the kinds of companies about which there is especially little known and which appeared underrepresented in our initial response. Clearly, with these sampling procedures, any attempt to make projections about "typical" practices in the private sector become problematic. The main compensating consideration, however, is that our discussion of policies in the selected industries can be more firmly based.

Of course our ability to make inferences about the population defined here rests on the "representativeness" of those responding to the survey. There can be no direct test of the sample's representativeness because relevant population parameters are unknown. We can only determine whether the returns constitute a random sample of the original sample—that is, whether there is a response bias.

By usual standards of what is satisfactory response for a mail survey in social science, 20 percent is low. (Including the telephone interviews, the overall response rate is 25 percent.) But it should be recognized that there is no statistical basis for determining whether a certain response rate is acceptable; at issue is the representativeness of those who do respond in terms of specific attributes.

First, we can consider the extent to which the distributions of companies in the sample approximate those of the response group for two key variables. These variables are: 1) industry, as indicated by the major categories in the Standard Industrial Classification, and 2) company size, as indicated by the number of employees. Previous research suggests that benefits provisions generally vary by company size and to some extent by industry.* These variables therefore seem essential to assessing the representativeness of the response group. (See tables A.1 and A.2.)

* Sheila B. Kamerman and Paul W. Kingston, "Employer Responses to the Family Responsibilities of Employees," in Sheila B. Kamerman and Cheryl B. Hayes, eds., *Families That Work: Children in a Changing World* (Washington, D.C.: National Academy Press, 1982).

**Table A.1.** Distributions by Industrial Category

| Industrial Category | Response Group * | Total Sample |
|---|---|---|
| Agriculture/mining construction | 8% | 12% |
| Manufacturing | 26 | 25 |
| Transportation/ communication | 8 | 7 |
| Trade | 22 | 27 |
| Finance | 32 | 26 |
| Service | 4 | 5 |
| | 100% | 100% (rounded) |

*Includes respondents to the mail and telephone surveys.

If the mail and telephone interviews are considered together, the distribution by industry type in the response group quite closely matches that in the sample. To a slight degree, the response group overrepresents financial firms and underrepresents firms in the combined category of agriculture-mining-construction as well as trade.

The results in table A.2 suggest that the response group underrepresents the very smallest firms (1–25 employees) and overrepresents those with 100–499 employees. To the extent, then, that these underrepresented firms offer relatively poor accom-

**Table A.2.** Distributions by Number of Employees

| Number of Employees | Response Group * | Total Sample |
|---|---|---|
| 1–25 | 23% | 31% |
| 26–99 | 28 | 32 |
| 100–499 | 30 | 22 |
| 500–999 | 5 | 4 |
| 1,000+ | 8 | 6 |
| Not available | 7 | 4 |
| | 100% (rounded) | 100% (rounded) |

*Includes respondents to the mail and telephone surveys.

modations for childbirth, *estimates based on this survey are likely to overstate the benefits provided by American businesses.* While responses may be weighted to correct the proportional representation by firm size, the general value of this procedure is slight given the substantial standard error associated with our estimates.

We can also attempt an indirect test of response bias by comparing the distribution of responses on certain important items in each mailing. The logic of making this assumption rests on a supposition: if there are any distinctive factors causing nonresponse, the relatively reluctant respondents (as indicated by the mailing to which they responded) should be more like the nonrespondents (the completely reluctant) in these respects than the willing respondents. For instance, one might imagine that firms with poor benefits are disproportionately inclined not to complete the questionnaire. However, one might also reasonably expect that the second mailing prompted a number of these firms to overcome their reluctance and complete the questionnaire. The proportion of companies with poor benefits (e.g., no disability insurance) would therefore increase from the first to the second mailing. Although the actual proportion of firms with a particular benefit is still indeterminate, it may be inferred that the completion of the questionnaire is related to the generosity of benefits and that analysis based on the response group overstates the level of benefits available to childbearing women.*

Table A.3 presents the distribution by mailing on six key benefits. The results do not have consistent implications. On the most basic matter of whether a firm provides a maternity leave of any kind, there is no difference between the companies in the first and second mailing. Companies in the second mailing appear relatively reluctant to grant a guarantee of a comparable job on return from leave (81 percent vs. 69 percent), though this difference is not statistically significant at the conventional .05 level. There is also not a statistically significant

---

*The telephone responses are excluded from this analysis because they are necessarily not representative of the remaining nonrespondents. Given the selection criteria for inclusion in the telephone survey, they may be expected to offer relatively poor benefits, and indeed they do generally offer lesser benefits.

**Table A.3.** Provision of Benefits, by Mailing

| Benefit | First Mailing | Follow-up Mailing |
|---|---|---|
| Maternal leave | 88% | 89% |
| Guarantee of comparable job on return | 81% | 69% |
| Disability insurance | 52% | 43% |
| Health insurance | 96% | 92% |
| Paid sick leave | 81% | 67%★ |
| Paternal leave | 29% | 12%★ |

★ Difference significant at .05 level.

difference at the .05 level on the provision of disability insurance (52 percent vs. 43 percent) or health insurance (96 percent vs. 92 percent). However, the companies in the second mailing are less likely to offer paid sick leave and any kind of paternal leave.

We emphasize that such analysis cannot establish the size of any response bias, but the results reported here do not indicate an overwhelming response bias. Together, the distributions of table A.3 suggest that the response group may overrepresent relatively generous firms to some degree. In light of this analysis and the previously noted underrepresentation of the smallest firms, it is clearly appropriate to make estimates with great caution. In general, as we will repeatedly note, our estimates probably tend to overstate the benefits available across the range of American businesses. Of course, since the sample is small, estimates based on this study must be considered rough approximations in any case.

## DESIGNING THE QUESTIONNAIRE

The main concern in designing the questionnaire was to include items that were appropriate for diverse kinds of companies. We could not reasonably expect executives at all companies—especially those without separate personnel departments—to be appraised of all relevant details, nor to be willing to give much time to completing the questionnaire. Accordingly, the questionnaire is fairly short, highlighting key concerns with closed-ended questions. A draft of the questionnaire was pretested with a small group of companies. (A facsimile of the questionnaire is included at the end of this appendix.)

A considerable number of items in the questionnaire replicate or approximate items in a 1978 Conference Board study. We included similar items for two reasons: (1) to have an external benchmark that can serve as a rough check on our results; and (2) to assess, if possible, whether there had been any changes in maternity policies in the large corporate sector since the 1978 legislation.

Even though our survey was in effect also pretested on the respondents to the Conference Board study, it appears in retrospect that we overestimated the sophistication of many respondents about personnel policies. Large firms often have executives—human resource officers and the like—specifically charged with personnel matters. For them, the questionnaire covers familiar concerns; they repeatedly deal with the issues involved and understand the distinctions that certain items probe. On the other hand, executives at many smaller firms often have to contend with a myriad of concerns. Personnel policies (if policies exist) receive only part of their attention and probably a minor part at that. As a result, a few of them may not have fully understood particular items (e.g., the distinction between paid sick leave and short-term disability insurance). Also, in their hurry to complete the questionnaire, they may have made some errors. We have the distinct impression, suggested by both the pattern of responses on the mail questionnaires and questions raised in the telephone interviews, that this was the case. Accordingly, at appropriate points in the text, we have added cautionary provisos when the findings appear to be affected by misinterpretations.

Any misinterpretations of questions do not seem likely to distort materially the major findings, but our experience suggests possible improvements to make in future research efforts. For one matter, the language of personnel professionals, which is commonly used in the corporate sector, is not always clear to managers in small business. Simple, nontechnical specifications of terms and careful pretesting with small business managers are needed. Also, many managers, again especially in small business, appear willing to give only a very limited amount of time to completing a questionnaire.* Even a modest number of questions appear to come at the cost of some hurried and inaccurate responses. Our experience suggests that any mail survey on this topic that goes to a cross-section of companies should be short and focused on only the key matters. Many managers do not know even the most rudimentary details of their insurance coverage, for example, and thus it is to little avail to probe such specific matters in a questionnaire. Moreover, the limited demands of a short questionnaire would likely increase the response rate.

A short questionnaire focused on a few key matters is well suited to telephone interviews. Our record of success with such interviews suggests the value of this strategy for future research. No companies refused our request for a telephone interview, and we had the opportunity to clear up any confusion that arose. Managers appeared more willing to give fifteen minutes on the telephone rather than fifteen minutes or so to a mail questionnaire.

Readers will themselves judge our fifteen on-site case studies. It is our own view that while no group of companies could be representative, the splendid access offered and the richness of the materials obtained added substantially to our understanding of maternity policies and our ability to interpret the survey results.

---

*Our limited pretest suggested that managers could complete the questionnaire in less than fifteen minutes.

# FACSIMILE

COLUMBIA UNIVERSITY

622 West 113th Street                                          New York, N.Y. 10025

## SURVEY OF MATERNITY BENEFITS AND LEAVES

### PRELIMINARY

1. Are your employee policies relating to pregnancy and maternity essentially uniform for all female personnel throughout all units of the company (i.e., all subsidiaries, divisions, and locations)?

    _____Yes      _____No

    IF YES:  Please skip to Section I.

    IF NO:   a) Do you have different policies for office and nonoffice personnel within any unit of the company?  _____Yes      _____No

             b) Do policies vary (for either or both types of employees) among units of the company?              _____Yes      _____No

How to Report: (companies without uniform policies)

   - *If you have different policies for office and nonoffice employees, please report on the policies which apply to the larger group.*

   - *Companies with more than one unit should report on policies within their largest unit - either those which apply to all personnel within this unit if there is no distinction between office and nonoffice personnel or those which apply to the larger group.*

             c) Please check the group of female employees to which your responses apply:

                 _____All office personnel within the company or its largest unit

                 _____All nonoffice personnel within the company or its largest unit

                 _____All personnel within the largest unit of the company

## I WORKING DURING PREGNANCY

1. Is the employee permitted to work right up to delivery if healthy and able to do the work?

    _____Yes      _____No

    IF NO:   How many weeks before the expected delivery must she stop working?  _____ Weeks

2. Do you require medical certification that it is safe for the pregnant employee to continue working?

             Certification by employee's personal doctor?      _____Yes      _____No
             Certification by company's medical department?    _____Yes      _____No

We acknowledge the permission of the Conference Board to use a substantial number of questions from A Conference Board Survey of Women's Employee Benefits, c 1976.

## II MATERNITY LEAVE

*1. Do you allow a leave before and/or immediately following childbirth? _____Yes _____No

    IF YES: Please complete below. IF NO: Skip to Section III

    *a) Do you formally guarantee that an employee on such leave may have the same or a comparable job on her return to work? _____Yes _____No
       IF YES: In what year was this policy established? 19_____

    b) Is a woman employee's seniority status maintained if she takes such a leave? _____Yes _____No

    c) Earliest time leave can start: _____Weeks before delivery

    d) Minimum employment to be eligible for leave: _____Months

    *e) Maximum leave granted: _____Months

    f) Doctor's certification of disability required for an extension? _____Yes _____No

2. Please roughly estimate the number of employees that started maternity leave at any time in 1979. _____Estimated number on maternity leave

3. Based on your experience in recent years, approximately what percentage of women who take maternity leave do you expect to return to work:

    _____0-24%    _____25-49%    _____50-74%    _____75-100%

    a) Has there been a notable increase in the proportion returning to work over the last five years or so? _____Yes _____No _____Don't know

4. If an employee takes a maternity leave for more than a month, does she continue to participate in the plans listed below?

| (Check one for each plan) | Life Insurance | Pension Plan | Health Insurance Employee | Dependent |
|---|---|---|---|---|
| Not a benefit to any employee | _____ | _____ | _____ | _____ |
| Not continued for employees during maternity leave | _____ | _____ | _____ | _____ |
| Continued benefit with employee contribution | _____ | _____ | _____ | _____ |
| Continued benefit with no employee contribution | _____ | _____ | _____ | _____ |

## III HEALTH INSURANCE AND MATERNITY

*1. Does your health insurance plan cover normal maternity for women employees? _____Yes _____No

    IF YES: Please complete below    IF NO: Skip to Section IV

    a) What special maximum benefits apply in maternity cases for:

| | Maximum Amount OR | No Special Dollar OR Limit | Days |
|---|---|---|---|
| *1) Hospitalization | $_____ | _____ | ____ |
| 2) Doctors' expense benefits | $_____ | _____ | |
| 3) Hospital and medical benefits combined | $_____ | _____ | |

    b) What special deductible amount applies in maternity cases (other than standard major medical or comprehensive medical plan deductible)? $_____ or _____None.

    *NOTE: Starred items were included in telephone survey.

## IV  PAID SICK LEAVE

*1.  Do you have an uninsured paid sick leave program (formal or informal) providing for "pay continuation" if an employee cannot work because of sickness?

_____Yes  _____No

IF NO:  Skip to Section V

2.  What is the minimum service requirement for paid sick leave eligibility?  _____Months

*  How many days of pay continuation are generally allowed an employee who just meets the minimum requirement?  _____Days of Pay

## V  ACCIDENT, SHORT TERM DISABILITY, AND SICKNESS INSURANCE

*1.  Do you have a plan that pays weekly benefits for essentially short-term, nonoccupational disabilities?

_____Yes  _____No

IF NO:  Skip to Section VI

2.  Indicate the waiting periods and maximum duration of benefits for the following types of disability.  *(If a waiting period or maximum does not apply, check "No Wait" or "No Limit" as appropriate.)*

| | Waiting Period | | Maximum Duration of Payments | |
|---|---|---|---|---|
| | Number of Days | No Wait | Number of Weeks | No Limit |
| a) Normal pregnancy, not hospitalized | _____ | _____ | _____ | _____ |
| b) Normal pregnancy, hospitalized | _____ | _____ | _____ | _____ |
| c) Complicated or pathological pregnancy, not hospitalized | _____ | _____ | _____ | _____ |
| d) Complicated or pathological pregnancy, hospitalized | _____ | _____ | _____ | _____ |

## VI  MATERNITY INCOME PLAN

*1.  Do you have a separate maternity income plan, that is, a plan that provides income to an employee who stops working due to pregnancy, *other than or in addition to paid sick leave plan or sickness and accident insurance?*

_____Yes  _____No

IF YES:*  In what year was this plan established?  19___

---

We would appreciate receiving a copy of your maternity income plan.

VII  FATHERS

   * 1.  Can a male employee take a leave with job protection for the purpose of child care?

       \_\_\_\_\_Yes    \_\_\_\_\_No

       IF YES:  In what year was this plan established? 19\_\_\_\_

    2.  Are male employees eligible for any benefits relating to the birth or care of a child
        (other than health insurance covering their wives)?  \_\_\_\_\_Yes    \_\_\_\_\_No

       IF YES: Describe briefly: _____

       _____

       _____

       _____


VIII  COMPANY CHARACTERISTICS

    1. Number of employees. *(Rough estimates are adequate.)*

|  | | Approximate<br>% women |
|---|---|---|
| Entire company (including all divisions) | | |
|    Number of office employees | _____ | _____ |
|    Number of nonoffice employees (i.e.,<br>   production, maintenance, operators, etc.) | _____ | _____ |
|   * Total number of employees | _____ | _____ |

    *If your responses to this questionnaire refer to a division or some other unit within
the company, roughly estimate the following:*

|  | | Approximate<br>% women |
|---|---|---|
|    Number of office employees within the unit | _____ | _____ |
|    Number of nonoffice employees within the unit | _____ | _____ |
|    Total number of unit employees | _____ | _____ |

    2.  Are the employees covered by this questionnaire represented by a union or unions?

       \_\_\_\_\_None are    \_\_\_\_\_1-24% are    \_\_\_\_\_25-74% are    \_\_\_\_\_75% or more are

   * 3.  Are your policies relating to maternity and pregnancy the result of collective bargaining?

       \_\_\_\_\_None are    \_\_\_\_\_Some are    \_\_\_\_\_All are

       IF SOME OR ALL:  Are they primarily based on an industry wide agreement?  \_\_\_\_\_Yes \_\_\_\_\_No


We would welcome any additional comments.

Thank you very much for your cooperation.

# NOTES

## 1. MATERNITY AND THE WORKING WOMAN

1. The data reported here are from various reports issued by the Bureau of Labor Statistics. See, for example, Beverly L. Johnson and Elizabeth Waldman, "Marital and Family Patterns of the Labor Force," *Monthly Labor Review*, (October 1981), vol. 104, no. 10; and Allyson Sherman Grossman, "More Than Half of All Children Have Working Mothers," *Monthly Labor Review* (February 1982), vol. 105, no. 2.

2. U.S. Bureau of the Census, *Current Population Reports*, Series P-20, No. 358, "Fertility of American Women, June 1979" (Washington, D.C.: GPO, 1980).

3. U.S. National Center for Health Statistics, *Patterns of Employment Before and After Childbirth* (Washington, D.C.: GPO, 1979), p. 13, table 14.

4. U.S. Bureau of the Census, *Current Population Reports*, Series P-20, No. 341, "Fertility of American Women, June 1978" (Washington, D.C.: GPO, 1979).

5. U.S. Bureau of the Census, Fertility Division, unpublished data for 1978. Data for 1981 can be found in *Current Population Reports*, Series P-20, no. 378, "Fertility of American Women: June 1981" (Washington, D.C.: GPO, 1983).

6. Jay Belsky, *In the Beginning* (New York: Columbia University Press, 1982), p. 7.

7. *Ibid.*, p. 23.

8. Louise Silverstein, "A Critical Review of Current Research on Infant Day Care," appendix A in Sheila B. Kamerman and Alfred J. Kahn, *Child Care, Family Benefits, and Working Parents* (New York: Columbia University Press, 1981).

9. For some selected studies of the significance of the first year of a child's life and the importance of the mother-child relationship, see Bettye M. Caldwell, "The Effects of Infant Care," and Leon J. Yarrow, "Separation from Parents During Early Childhood," in Martin L. Hoffman and Lois W. Hoffman, eds., *Review of Child Development Research*, vol. 1 (New York: Russell Sage Foundation, 1964); Mary D. S. Ainsworth, "The Development of Infant-Mother Attachment," in Bettye M. Caldwell and Henry N. Ricciuti, eds.,

*Review of Child Development Research*, II (Chicago: University of Chicago Press, 1966); Burton L. White, *The First Three Years of Life* (Englewood Cliffs, N.J.: Prentice-Hall, 1975); Alison Clarke-Stewart, *Child Care in the Family*, (New York: Academic Press, 1977).

10. For some discussion of the policy trends in other countries, see Sheila B. Kamerman and Alfred J. Kahn, *Child Care, Family Benefits, and Working Parents*.

11. This section draws on material included in greater detail in Sheila B. Kamerman, *Maternity and Parental Benefits and Leaves: An International Review* (New York: Columbia University Center for the Social Sciences, 1980).

12. See *Child Care, Family Benefits, and Working Parents*. See also Sheila B. Kamerman and Alfred J. Kahn, *Family Policy: Government and Families in Fourteen Countries* (New York: Columbia University Press, 1978).

## 2. HISTORICAL NOTES ON MATERNITY POLICIES IN THE UNITED STATES

1. *New York Times*, September 22, 1981.

2. Wendy W. Williams, associate professor, Georgetown University Law Center, Testimony, U.S. Senate, Subcommittee on Labor of the Committee on Human Resources, *Discrimination on the Basis of Pregnancy*, 1977 (Report of Hearings) (Washington, D.C.: GPO, 1977), p. 123. The review of the history of maternity policies in the United States draws heavily on this testimony and material on the history of maternity protection in the United States in an unpublished paper by Anita Weinberg.

3. Sheila Lewenhab, *Women and Work* (Glasgow, Scotland: Fontana Paperbacks, 1980).

4. Josephine Goldmark, *Fatigue and Efficiency: A Study in Industry* (Philadelphia: Russell Sage Foundation, 1912), p. 318.

5. *Muller v. Oregon*, 208, U.S. 412 (1908).

6. Quoted in Williams, Testimony, p. 123.

7. Judge Learned Hand, *Ritchie and Co. v. Wayman*, 244 Ill. 509 (1910), quoted in Elizabeth Faulkner Baker, *Protective Labor Legislation: With Special Reference to Women in the State of New York* (New York: Columbia University Press, 1925), p. 68.

8. Goldmark, pp. 305–319.

9. Quoted in Williams, Testimony, p. 124.

10. Gwendolyn Salisbury Hughes, *Mothers in Industry: Wage Earnings by Mothers in Philadelphia* (New York: New Republic, 1925).

11. "Standards for Maternity Care and Employment of Mothers in Industry," July 1942.

12. U.S. Department of Labor, Women's Bureau, *Maternity Protection of Employed Women*, Bulletin no. 240 (Washington, D.C.: GPO, 1952), pp. 5–6.

13. Charlotte Silverman, M.D., "Maternity Policies in Industry," *The Child* (August 1943), 8(2):20–24.

14. Williams, Testimony, pp. 127–128.

15. *American Women*. Report of the President's Commission on the Status of Women (Washington, D.C.: GPO, 1963).

16. Esther Peterson, "Working Women," in Robert Jay Lifton, ed., *The Woman in America* (Boston: Beacon Press, 1964), p. 162.

17. Martha Derthick, *Policy Making for Social Security* (Washington, D.C.: The Brookings Institution, 1979), p. 26.

18. U.S. Department of Labor, Women's Bureau, *Maternity Benefit Provision*, Bulletin no. 272 (Washington, D.C.: GPO, 1960).

19. Williams, Testimony, p. 129.

20. Section 703 (a) (i).

21. For some discussion of this point, see Geraldine Leshin, *EEOC Law: Impact on Fringe Benefits* (Los Angeles: UCLA Institute of Industrial Relations, 1979).

22. *Ibid.*, p. 15.

23. The opinion letters are quoted in Leshin, *EEOC Law*, and have extracted conclusions from the Supreme Court decision in *Gilbert* v. *General Electric*, 429 U.S. 125 (1976).

24. *Ibid.*

25. *Gedulig* v. *Aiello*, 417 U.S. 484 (1974).

26. 434 U.S. 136 (1977). We have not attempted here a full legal history or a review of all legal issues. For interpretation from several ideological vantage points, see the following:

Nancy Erickson, "Pregnancy Discrimination: An Analytical Approach," *Women's Rights Reporter* (Winter/Spring 1979), 5(2–3):83–105.

Ann Corinne Hill, "Protection of Women Workers and the Courts: A Legal Case History," *Feminist Studies* (Summer 1979), 5(2):247–273. The major pregnancy cases as discussed, 265–273.

Richard Marshall Abrams, "Primary and Secondary Characteristics in Discrimination Cases, *Villanova Law Review* (November 1977), 23(1):35–67. Pregnancy as a "sex-linked" characteristic is discussed on pp. 38–40.

Susan Chastain, "Notes: Pregnancy and Disability Insurance," *Drake Law Review* (November 1974), 23(4):804–819.

Patricia M. Lines, "Update: New Rights for Pregnant Employees," *Personnel Journal* (January 1979), pp. 33–37.

27. Nancy Erikson, "Pregnancy Discrimination: An Analytical Approach," p. 102.

28. A 1978 report of a 1976 survey indicates that although 90 percent of the workers were covered by employment-related health insurance plans, "3 out of 5 workers in plans with maternity benefits could anticipate less protection for normal delivery pregnancy expenses than for expenses due to other

reasons." Dorothy R. Kittner, "Maternity Benefits Available to Most Health Plan Participants," *Monthly Labor Review* (May 1972).

29. *Discrimination Based on Pregnancy*, 1972.

## 3. THE BENEFIT PICTURE: EMPLOYEE AND EMPLOYER PERSPECTIVES

1. U.S. Department of Labor Management Services, Pension Advice and Welfare Benefit Program, "Group Health Insurance Coverage of Private Full Time Wage and Salary Workers, 1979" (Washington, D.C.: GPO, 1981).

2. Congress of the United States, Congressional Budget Office, *Profile of Health Care Coverage: The Haves and the Have Nots* (Washington, D.C.: GPO, 1979).

3. Sheila B. Kamerman and Paul W. Kingston, "Employer Responses to the Family Responsibilities of Employees," in Sheila B. Kamerman and Cheryl B. Hayes, eds., *Families That Work: Children in a Changing World of Work, Family and Community* (Washington, D.C.: National Academy Press, 1982).

4. Robert P. Quinn and Graham L. Staines, *The 1977 Quality of Employment Survey: Descriptive Statistics, with Comparison Data from the 1969–70 and 1972–73 Surveys* (Ann Arbor, Mich.: Institute for Social Research, 1979).

The results reported here and elsewhere in this book are based on the 1977 cross-section sample. (Surveys in 1969 and 1972 are useful for trend analysis; also available is a 1973–77 panel study). The 1977 survey has 1,515 respondents; it is a nationally representative sample of all employed adults, age 16 or older, currently employed for twenty hours or more per week. The 1977 survey includes the "core" material of the preceding surveys—earnings and fringe benefits, work task and job content, working hours and attitudes toward various aspects of work. In addition, it includes new items relating to the employment of the spouse and the impact of employment on family life.

5. A 1978 Conference Board study provides the most detailed analysis of practices in the large corporate sector: Mitchell Meyer, *Women and Employer Benefits* (New York: Conference Board, 1978). Though details on the sample are sparse, the 309 firms in the sample are almost all drawn from the ranks of the larger corporations. Moreover, since many companies were included in the sample simply because of long-standing ties with the Conference Board, it is impossible to claim that the responding companies are representative of even the large corporations, much less American business in general.

6. Equal Employment Opportunity Commission, "Guidelines on Discrimination Because of Sex," 1972 (processed).

7. Kamerman and Kingston, "Employer Responses." This review includes an analysis of the QES, as well as a synthesis of findings from a number of employee- and employer-focused studies.

8. Catalyst Career and Family Center, *Corporations and Two-Career Families* (New York: Catalyst, 1981).

9. *Ibid.*

10. Hewitt Associates, in Kamerman and Kingston, "Employer Responses."

11. Senator Birch Bayh, Testimony, U.S. Senate subcommittee on labor of the Committee on Human Resources, "Discrimination on the Basis of Pregnancy," 95th Congress, 1st sess. (Washington, D.C.: GPO, 1977).

12. Kamerman and Kingston's "Employer Responses" includes data from a special analysis of QES.

13. See Kamerman and Kingston, "Employer Responses," for a report of data concerning other benefits. See appendix for a discussion of the representativeness biases in use of the Dunn and Bradstreet directories.

14. U.S. Department of Labor, Bureau of Labor Statistics, *News*, "Labor Organization Membership . . . 1980s," September 3, 1981, reports that 24.5 percent of the total nonagricultural labor force is unionized. Only about 16 percent of the private labor force is unionized.


## 4. THE BENEFIT PICTURE: STATE AND FEDERAL PROVISIONS

1. Personal communication.

2. "Statement of New York Senator Carole Bellamy in Support of Legislation Amending Title VII to Prohibit Discrimination Against Pregnant Workers."

3. Patricia K. Putnam, Associate Dean for Legal and Legislative Affairs, School of Medicine of the University of Hawaii, Honolulu, Testimony, U.S. Senate subcommittee on labor of the Committee on Human Resources, "Discrimination on the Basis of Pregnancy," 95th Congress, 1st sess. (Washington, D.C.: GPO, 1977).

4. Daniel N. Price, "Cash Benefits for Short-Term Sickness, 1979," *Social Security Bulletin* (September 1982), 45(9):15–19.

5. U.S. Office of Personnel Management, *Federal Facts: Maternity Benefits of the Federal Employee* (Washington, D.C.: GPO, 1980).

6. U.S. Personnel Manual, "Absence for Maternity Reasons."


## 6. MATERNITY POLICIES: TRENDS AND ISSUES

1. QES, p. 60, table 4.13.

2. Linda Hamilton Clinton, "Working Mothers with Infants and Toddlers: How They Manage," *Working Mothers*, September 1981. Almost two-thirds of the women surveyed were back at work within three months after delivery, but nine out of ten thought that was too soon, according to the findings of this study. Asked what the ideal maternity leave would be, half answered six months and 38 percent chose one year.

In a survey carried out by *Parents* magazine (October 1982), the results were similar. Almost 95 percent of the respondents had children under age 3 and of these, more than half were in the labor force (52 percent). Almost half returned to work in less than three months and 71 percent in less than six months.

3. U.S. National Center for Health Statistics, Larry A. Bumpass and James A. Sweet, *Patterns of Employment Before and After Childbirth* (Hyattsville, Md.: USDHEW, Public Health Service, 1980).

4. For 1978 data, see U.S. Bureau of the Census, *Current Population Reports*, Series P-20, No. 341, "Fertility of American Women, June 1978" (Washington, D.C.: GPO, 1979). Data for 1981 were provided by Dr. Martin O'Connell, Chief, Fertility Division, U.S. Bureau of the Census.

5. U.S. Department of Labor, *Group Health Insurance Coverage of Private Full Time Wage and Salary Workers, 1979* (Washington, D.C.: Management Services Administration, Pension and Welfare Benefit Programs, 1981), processed.

6. U.S. Congress, Congressional Budget Office, *Profile of Health Care Coverage: The Haves and the Have Nots* (Washington, D.C.: GPO, 1979).

7. For the limitations on coverage, even among working women, see table 3.2.

8. Gerry E. Hendershot, "Work During Pregnancy and Subsequent Hospitalization of Mothers and Infants," *Public Health Reports: Child and Family Health* (September–October 1979), 94(5):425–426.

9. See, for example, U.S. Bureau of the Census, *Current Population Reports*, Series P-23, no. 110, "Characteristics of Households and Persons Receiving Noncash Benefits:1979" (Washington, D.C.: GPO, 1981).

10. See Daniel N. Price, "Cash Benefits for Short Term Sickness, 1979," *Social Security Bulletin* (September 1982), 45(9):15–19.

11. William E. Easterling, Jr., "The Puerperium." In David N. Danforth, ed., *Obstetrics and Gynecology*, 3d ed. (Hagerstown, Md.: Harper and Row, 1977).

12. See Sheila B. Kamerman and Alfred J. Kahn, *Child Care, Family Benefits, and Working Parents* (New York: Columbia University Press, 1981), ch. 5.

# INDEX

Adoption, 23, 62-63, 124-25
AFL-CIO, 33, 45
American Federation of Labor, *see* AFL-CIO

Bayh, Senator Birch, 66
Bellamy, Carol, 44
Belsky, Jay, 13

California, 41, 83-86, 98, 115-17
Cash benefits, 3, 14, 30, 47, 139-41; *see also* Paid leaves
Chamber of Commerce, 45
Child care, *see* Children
Child development, *see* Children
Children, 156; care of, 145-46; importance of first year of life, 12-14; needs of, 46, 145-46, 151; with working mothers, 8
Children's Bureau, 34, 35
Civil Rights Act of 1964, Title VII, 38-43, 46
Columbia University Survey, 54-63, 67-74, 161-73
Comparable job, 108-11, 138, 144
Conference Board, 53-54, 55-59 *passim*, 65, 66, 73
Costs of maternity benefits, 129-30; as estimated in 1977, 45
Court cases, *see* Supreme Court; *see also under specific cases*
Coverage (overall picture), 96-98; *see also* Disability insurance; Health insurance; Sickness benefits

Definition (maternity policies), 3, 4
Disability: before childbirth, 53-54, 105, 119, 145, 150; at childbirth, 44-45, 119; after childbirth, 142, 144, 151; medical standard, 142-43
Disability insurance, 44-45, 63, 68-72, 75, 96-98, 111, 113-20, 139-41, 143, 150; coverage, 96-98, 139-41; Temporary Disability Insurance, 77-95, 97-98, 115-17, 139-40, 143, 150
Discrimination, *see* Pregnancy Discrimination Act; Sex discrimination

Employers: expectations, 73-74; perspectives, 54-74, 126-31, 147-49; problems, 147-49
Employment, *see* Labor force participation
Equal Employment Opportunity Commission (EEOC), 39-43, 53-54, 138, 155
Equal rights, *see* Equal Employment Opportunities Commission; Sex discrimination

Fathers, 23, 62; *see also* Paternity benefits and leaves
Federal government, as employer, 95-96
Friedan, Betty, 152
Futter, Ellen, 29

*Gedulig v. Aiello,* 41, 177*n*
*Gilbert v. General Electric Corporation,* 40-41
Gompers, Samuel, 33
Government, 155-59; *see also* Federal government; State governments

Hand, Judge Learned, 32
Hawaii, 44, 93-94

Health insurance, 3, 14, 37, 43, 47-50, 51, 60, 74-75, 106, 136-37; availability of, 49-51; coverage, 48-50, 74-75; importance of, 136-37; operating picture, 101-4

Health Insurance Association of America, 45

History, 1-2, 29-46, 145, 155

Implementation (maternity policies), 99-131

Importance (maternity policies), 5, 6-14, 134-36

International Labor Organization (ILO), 15, 30, 31, 145

Job-protected leaves, 3, 47, 50-54, 56-62, 75, 137-39; availability, 56-58, 60-62; coverage, 75; operating picture, 108-11; see also Comparable job; Leaves; Paid leaves; Unpaid leaves

Leaves, 3, 14, 47, 56-75, 137-39; availability, 56; length, 57-59, 105, 117-20; mandatory, 36, 37; operating picture, 104-20; see also Job-protected leaves; Paid leaves; Unpaid leaves; Sickness benefits

Managers' perspectives, 1-2, 120-22, 131, 154-55, 157

Maternity policies: definition of, 3, 4; history of, 29-46; implementation, 99-131; importance of, 5, 6-14, 134-36; in other countries, 4, 14-25, 30, 31, 118, 133-34, 145, 148-49, 153, 155-56; as protective legislation, 30, 31-33, 34-35, 36; as sex discrimination, 38-43; strategies for the U.S., 148, 149-60; trends and issues, 133-60; in the U.S., 4, 31, 45-46, 77; see also specific maternity policies such as Disability insurance; Health insurance; Paid leaves; Trends and issues; Unpaid leaves

Muller v. Oregon, 32, 176n

Nashville Gas Co. v. Satty, 41

National Survey of Family Growth, 137

New Jersey, 45, 86-90

New York, 44, 45, 90-93

Other countries (maternity policies), 4, 14-25, 30, 31, 118, 133-34, 145, 148-49, 153, 155-56

Packaging maternity benefits, 122, 143

Paid leaves, 63-74, 75-76, 143; length, 117-20; operating picture, 111-20; see also Disability insurance; Sickness benefits

Paid sick leave, see Sickness benefits

Parental benefits and leaves, 104; in other countries, 23, 153; see also Parenting; Paternity benefits and leaves

Parenting, 145-46, 155; see also Parental benefits and leaves

Paternity benefits and leaves, 62, 104, 124-25; in other countries, see Parental benefits and leaves

Part-time workers, 48, 74, 124-25, 155

Pregnancy and maternity: defined as temporary disabilities, 46, 69, 142; and disability, 53-54, 105, 119, 145, 150; and discrimination, 41-43; and work, 11-12

Pregnancy Disability Amendment, see Pregnancy Discrimination Act

Pregnancy Discrimination Act, 41-43, 63, 139, 155

President's Commission on the Status of Women, 36

Protective legislation (maternity policies as), 30, 31-33, 34-35, 36

Puerperium, 142

Quality of Employment Survey, 48, 52-53, 55, 64-66, 97

Rhode Island, 78-83

Ritchie & Co. v. Wayman, 32, 176n

Seniority rights, 108-9

Sex discrimination, 38-43, 46, 141-42, 144, 150

Sickness benefits, 54, 67-68, 71, 140-41, 142, 143, 150

Small employers, 49, 52, 57, 140, 148

State governments, 32-33, 77-95, 96-98; as employer, 94

Strategies (for maternity policies), 148, 149-60

Supreme Court, 32, 35, 38, 40, 41

Temporary Disability Insurance (TDI), 77-95, 97-98, 115-17, 139-40, 142-43, 150, 158-59

Title VII of the Civil Rights Act of 1964, *see* Civil Rights Act

Trends and issues, 3, 5, 25-27, 74-76, 96-98, 133-60

Unions, 71, 153-54, 156-57

U.S. maternity policy, 4, 31, 45-46, 77

Unpaid leaves: availability of, 56-57, 65-66; coverage, 75; operating picture, 104-11; *see also* Job-protected leaves

Unemployment Insurance, 37

Vacations, 107, 141, 143

Williams, Wendy, 29, 37, 176*n*

Women: contributing to family income, 10-11; fertility rates, 8-10; in the labor force, 7-8, 9, 135, 156; returning to work after childbirth, 11, 59, 125, 142-43, 151; working while pregnant, 11-12

Women's Bureau, 34

Women's organizations, 152-53